I0824585

Advance Praise

"We can't change what we can't talk about. And what we don't talk about creates what Gustavo Razzetti calls 'Conversational Debt' which compounds into teams that spin and fail to move forward. This book will help you unravel what is holding you, your relationships, and teams back from breaking through to the next level."

—**GREG MCKEOWN,** *New York Times* bestselling author of *Essentialism*, *Effortless*, and *The Essentialism Planner*

"This book names a hidden problem most leaders face: conversational debt—and shows how to break free from it."

—**TASHA EURICH,** *New York Times* bestselling author of *Shatterproof*, *Insight*, and *Bankable Leadership*

"Gustavo doesn't sugarcoat team dynamics. *Forward Talk* reflects the same bold, practical approach he brings to real conversations—naming what people avoid and helping teams move forward without blame or theatrics. The shift was visible: tougher topics surfaced earlier, peers challenged each other with respect instead of retreating, and trust climbed because people could finally see that their voice had agency and moved the work forward."

—**TOM LEEMANS,** Global Ice Cream Director, Mars Wrigley

"*Forward Talk* is a must-read for every leader who's tired of their team crumbling under the weight of unspoken concerns and unresolved conflicts. Razzetti has created an accessible guide that shows you how to draw out honesty and alignment in conversations to drive better results."

—**MELODY WILDING,** LMSW, author of *Managing Up*

"*Forward Talk* works great for people who might be scared to speak, as it gives them a way of reframing that doesn't abruptly challenge the status quo."

—**ASTHA LAGOO**, Sr. Program Manager, Google

"*Forward Talk* names something many leaders feel but struggle to articulate: the slow disengagement that happens when people stop believing their voice matters. Gustavo Razzetti gives us language for that cost and, more importantly, a practical framework for breaking the conversational patterns that keep teams stuck. This is a book about how teams regain momentum through better conversations."

—**TAMARA MYLES,** author of *Meaningful Work*

"*Forward Talk* is a rare mix of honesty and practicality. It goes beyond communication techniques to address the real issue: why capable people disengage conversationally. The book captures the messy reality of team conversations and offers a clear, practical, experience-tested path to shift from silence, false harmony, and blame toward conversations that actually change things."

—**EMANUELE MAZZANTI**, Leadership Development and Facilitation, Ernst & Young

"Razzetti brilliantly captures a truth I've witnessed countless times: Teams often fail not because people lack talent, but because they avoid the conversations that matter most. *Forward Talk* offers leaders practical tools to build what every effective team needs—the courage and skill to address what's really going on and then move forward. If you want to lead a team that thrives on productive conflict rather than polite avoidance, this book is essential reading."

—**AMY GALLO,** Contributing Editor at *Harvard Business Review* and author of *Getting Along*

"Gustavo Razzetti nails something most leaders miss: People don't stay silent because they're afraid; they stay silent because they think speaking up won't matter. *Forward Talk* shows how small, practical shifts can replace polite stagnation with trust, clarity, and momentum. You won't sit silently through a pointless meeting again."

—**DANIEL H. PINK,** #1 *New York Times* bestselling author of *The Power of Regret* and *Drive*

"Teams often assume that speaking up won't change the status quo, creating what Gustavo Razzetti calls conversational debt: unspoken concerns, avoided truths, and circular discussions that stall progress. Gustavo piloted this methodology with our leadership cohort. In a large, decentralized institution like ours, communication often gets diluted across colleges and administrative layers.

His Forward Talk framework breaks that cycle. It gives leaders a practical way to move beyond blame, avoidance, and groupthink while strengthening trust. It's not just another tool—it's a courageous, transformative way of leading that helps teams surface real issues and create meaningful forward momentum."

—**TRICIA BACHUS,** Sr. Leadership and Organizational Development Specialist, University of Florida

"*Forward Talk* goes beyond concepts like psychological safety and team cohesion by providing actionable ways to improve team conversations. This book helps teams get out of the swirl and start moving forward."

—**ALLISON HOWELL,** CEO, Hogan Assessments

"Most teams don't fail because they lack talent. They fail because they avoid the conversations that matter most. *Forward Talk* gives leaders a clear, practical system for turning silence and tension into alignment, ownership, and real progress."

—**NIR EYAL,** author of *Indistractable* and *Beyond Belief*

"Unlocking bold leadership requires someone with an unwavering commitment to clarity of vision and positive change to guide our journey. With a relentless focus on simplifying challenges, fostering shared ownership, and tackling tough decisions head-on, Gustavo and his Forward Talk approach inspired us to move beyond excuses and perfectionism."

—**JAMES P. SCRIVEN,** CEO, IDB Invest

"*Forward Talk* changed how I think about difficult conversations. It's practical and clear, and it teaches leaders how to move through discomfort in a way that builds accountability, trust, and forward movement on the issues that matter most."

—**HYLA POLLAK,** Fractional HR Leader (Canada)

"*Forward Talk* helps leaders reclaim their conversational agency and break cycles of avoidance, blame, and groupthink. Gustavo Razzetti provides practical tools to create future-focused conversations that move work and culture forward. A must-read for any leader committed to building a team where courage, agency, and collaboration are lived every day."

—**EWA HUTMACHER,** CEO and Cofounder, Snabbfoting (Sweden)

"*Forward Talk* is an outstanding seminal work. Gustavo's principles, frameworks, and actionable insights will bring leaders and coaches greater fluency, competence, and confidence, even courage, when navigating the breakthroughs often required to building purposeful high-impact relationships, teams, and cultures."

—**PAUL O'KELLY,** Founder, Mylyn (Ireland)

Also by Gustavo Razzetti

Remote Not Distant

Stretch for Change

Stretch Your Mind

Forward Talk

Forward Talk

THE BOLD NEW METHOD FOR GETTING TEAMS UNSTUCK

Gustavo Razzetti

IDEAPRESS PUBLISHING
WASHINGTON, DC

Ideapress Publishing | www.ideapresspublishing.com

Cover Design: Catherine Casalino
Interior Design: Jessica Angerstein
Visual Images: Janis Ozolins

Cataloging-in-Publication Data is on file with the Library of Congress.

Hardcover ISBN: 978-1-64687-247-3

---

1 2 3 4 5 6 7 8 9 10

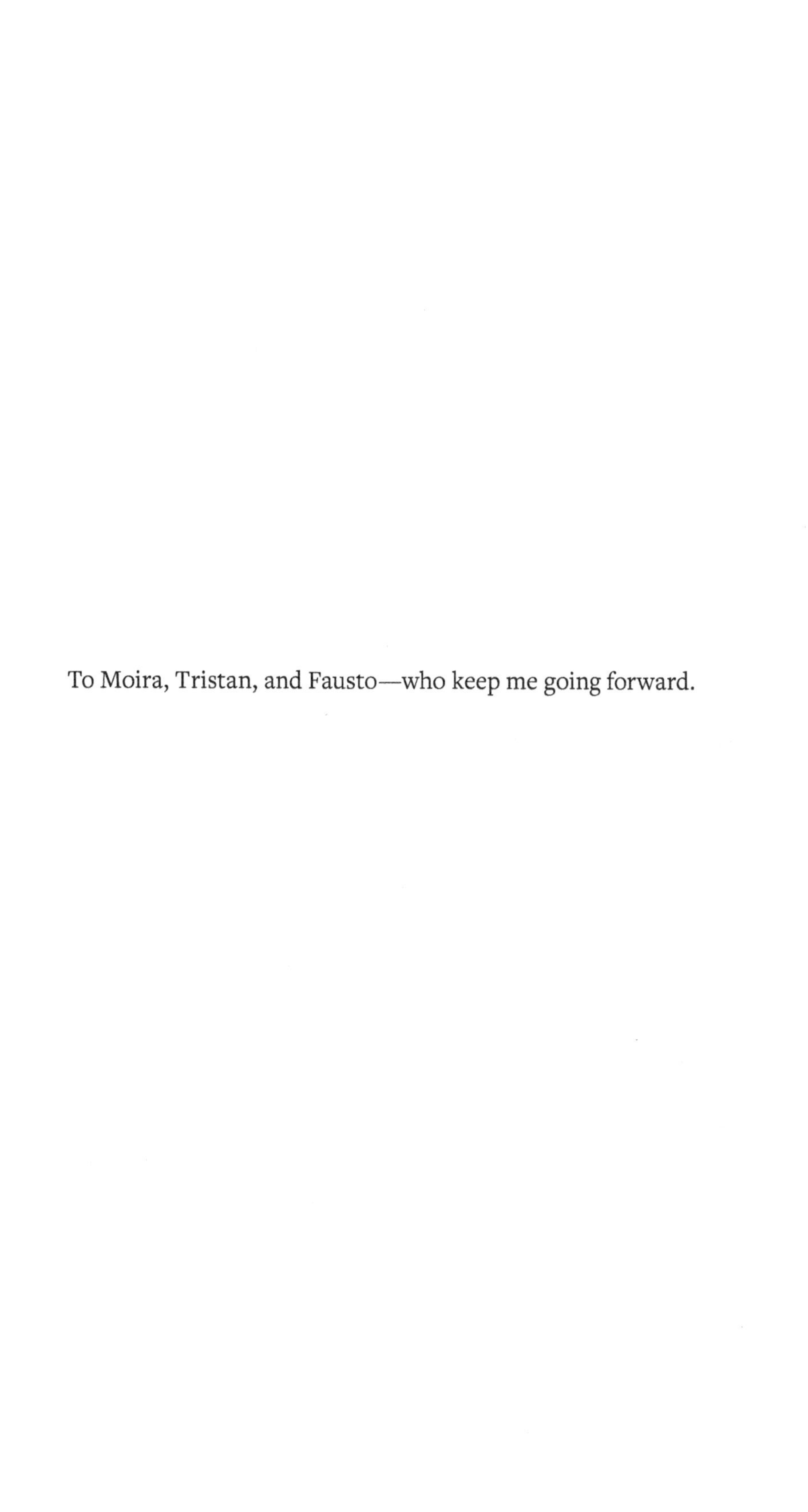

To Moira, Tristan, and Fausto—who keep me going forward.

Contents

Introduction

Your team's success isn't determined by how hard people work. It's determined by the quality of your conversations—especially the ones you're not having.

Every day, teams accumulate conversational debt: a concern left unspoken, a rushed decision, a conflict smoothed over rather than addressed. Like financial debt, it starts small, but eventually the bill comes due.

I've spent my career watching smart people make foolish decisions together—not because they lack talent or good intentions, but because the critical conversations never happened.

That's why I wrote this book: to help you avoid the same costly mistakes.

"Forward Talk" offers a new way to improve team conversations. I've spent nearly two decades building and testing this method with real teams—including my own.

If you want a book about "difficult conversations," there are hundreds. Most are so structured that you'd need a coaching certification to use them. I promise to keep this book actionable without turning you into a team therapist.

This isn't another psychological safety manual either, focused on creating safe spaces. The truth is, waiting for perfect conditions only makes things worse.

My research instead reveals a surprising truth: People often stay silent not because they're afraid, but because they don't believe speaking up will change anything.

Most leaders were never taught to facilitate conversations—they were taught to dominate them. They learned to have all the answers, not to unlock the collective intelligence already in the room. Facilitation—drawing out diverse perspectives to reach breakthrough thinking—is one of the most overlooked leadership skills.[1]

This book helps teams break the patterns that get teams stuck—blame, avoidance, and groupthink—and shows how to have conversations that drive real progress. I've tested Forward Talk with multiple organizations, including Microsoft, Mars, the University of Florida, IDB Invest, Merck, and Globant. The results speak for themselves.

You don't need a formal title to apply this framework. Whether you're leading a team, facilitating change, or simply tired of meetings that go nowhere, this book will teach you how to spot conversational debt, interrupt destructive patterns, and build habits with lasting momentum. The best teams don't avoid conflict—they address the issues in the room.

Effective conversations aren't easy or tension-free. Forward Talk requires courage, curiosity, and commitment. But it delivers what most teams rarely experience: real progress instead of endless circling.

With the right approach, your team can manage, reduce, and even prevent conversational debt. You'll learn how to surface disagreement more effectively, drive real alignment, and make smarter, faster decisions.

The stories in this book aren't polished case studies where everything works perfectly. That's intentional. Real teams are messy. Real conversations go sideways before they get better. But once you have the right tools, when your own conversations get messy—and they will—you'll know what to do next. Real breakthrough happens when people stop performing and start being honest.

You can only improve what you actually talk about. It's time to stop accumulating the cost of silence and start building conversational wealth. Are you ready to make the change?

Before You Continue

Throughout this book, you'll find practical insights and exercises to help you improve your team's conversations.

To make it easier for you, I've put together some free tools to help you get started:

- Ready-to-use templates for better conversations
- A quick quiz to assess your conversational debt
- Extra resources and tips

Go to gustavorazzetti.com/forward-talk-tools
or scan the QR code below.

How to Explore This Book

I don't read books in order—except for novels. Instead, I go straight to what I'm looking for. So while you're certainly welcome to, I don't expect you to read mine from start to finish.

Rather, I've designed this book like a toolkit. Grab exactly what you need, when you need it. Below I've outlined different ways to navigate the sections depending on your team challenges.

What's Inside

This book draws on my twenty-five years of facilitating conversations with teams in Fortune 500 companies, startups, and organizations in over thirty countries. It's backed by research with more than five thousand professionals and qualitative insights from over fifteen hundred workshops helping senior executives, team members, and coaches improve their conversations.

Within these pages, you'll learn how to:

- Spot the three Backward Talk conversational patterns (blame, avoidance, and groupthink) that trap teams

- Pinpoint exactly where your team is accumulating conversational debt and why it compounds
- Build the courage your team needs to address real issues before they become bigger
- Use strategic interventions to transform how your team communicates
- Facilitate conversations that unlock collective intelligence
- Prevent conversational debt from reaccumulating with simple practices

Book Overview

Part I: Stuck in Backward Talk

The foundation + immediate action tools.

Learn why teams get trapped in Backward Talk conversational patterns: blame, avoidance, and groupthink. You'll get techniques to reframe conversations in real time. Plus, you'll learn how to use the "Breaking the Conversational Loop Canvas" to map which destructive patterns your team repeats most often.

Part II: Break Free from Debt

Diagnose what's really going wrong.

Discover how unaddressed conversations accumulate as debt across three areas: alignment (false agreement), belonging (artificial harmony), and collaboration (lack of resolution). Use the "Conversational Debt Spiral Canvas" to identify your team's specific patterns and where to focus your efforts.

Part III: Reclaim Your Voice

Build courage and transform team dynamics.

Learn why people surrender their conversational agency and how they can reclaim it. You'll explore the "CPR Framework" (Courage, Perspective, Responsibility) and uncover tools to help individuals reclaim their agency. Plus, you'll learn how to use the "CPR Canvas" to help teams shift from powerless to powerful roles.

Part IV: Move Forward

Your strategic implementation playbook.

Get systematic approaches for deeper transformation: strategic solutions and prevention methods. Use the "Forward Talk Canvas" to navigate difficult conversations as a team.

Dive Into the Book

You can explore this book in the order it was written, or dive into the section that's more relevant to your team's needs. Here are three ways you can explore it from shallow to deepest:

How to Explore This Book

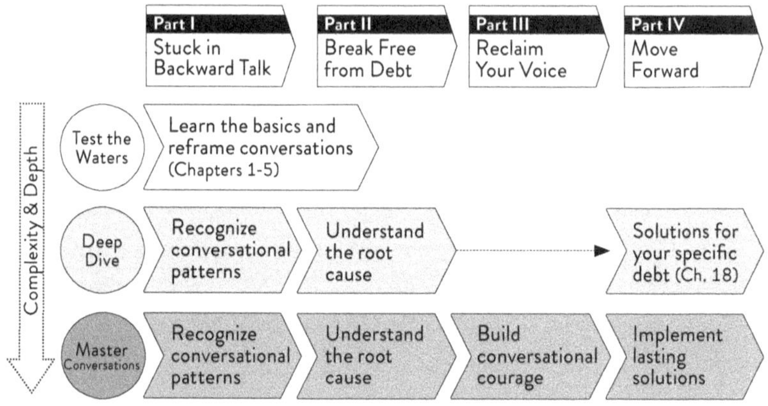

1. Test the Waters

Chapters 1–5

When to use it: You want to try a few quick interventions and see how they resonate with your team.

How it works: Learn the foundation and try conversation reframes in your next meeting to shift from Backward Talk to Forward Talk.

What you get: Select from twenty-five curated conversational reframes that match your team's everyday challenges.

Bonus points if you read Chapter 6 and test the "Breaking the Conversational Loop Canvas" with your team, mapping most common patterns.

2. Deep Dive

Part I: Stuck in Backward Talk → Part II: Break Free from Debt → Chapter 18: Forward Talk Practices

When to use it: You want to identify and address the underlying causes of your team's communication breakdowns.

How it works: Learn the foundation, diagnose specific debt patterns, understand why they developed, and then dive deep into strategic solutions.

What you get: Uncover a complete diagnostic system plus strategic exercises matched to your team's specific conversational debt.

3. Master Conversations

Part I: Stuck in Backward Talk → Part II: Break Free from Debt → Part III: Reclaim Your Voice → Part IV: Move Forward

When to use it: You want to fundamentally solve your team's communication problems and prevent them from happening again.

How it works: This is the approach I use with consulting clients—an intentional sequence that peels back each layer of the conversational onion: recognizing destructive patterns, understanding why they persist, building the courage to change them, and finally implementing lasting solutions.

What you get: You'll learn a complete system to master courageous conversations and cancel conversational debt for good. It includes the four canvases and multiple interventions, from simple conversational reframes to more complex solutions.

My Recommendation

Feel free to dive straight into the tools in Chapter 18 or the conversational reframes in Chapter 5, or whatever path you want to explore. But I strongly recommend reading Chapters 2 and 3 first. Understanding why conversations derail, how conversational debt accumulates, and what Forward Talk looks like will make the tools far more effective. It's like mastering the fundamentals—learning how to swim close to shore before heading further out. The diagnostic canvases and interventions are more powerful once you grasp the principles behind them.

Once you've covered the basics, follow your curiosity. Try what resonates. Skip what doesn't fit your needs. Explore this book in whatever way works best for you.

A word of caution: Some tools require skilled external facilitators, particularly when you're just starting or if you're unsure if your team is ready. Courageous conversations require hard work. Begin in the shallows and gradually build your confidence before venturing into deeper waters.

Real Stories, Not Fiction

Most business books share perfect case studies. They sound inspiring but don't match real life. Reality is often messier and more complex, leaving you frustrated with the stories.

This book is different. I'm sharing real stories from my work as both a consultant and leader because:

They're authentic. I lived these situations.

They feel familiar. You'll think, *I've seen that happen.*

They show the path. I won't show you just the finish line, but how people got there.

They give hope. If these ideas worked in messy places, they can work for you.

They're practical. You'll see what to try, what to avoid, and how to adapt solutions to your reality.

Ready? Let's dive in.

PART I

Stuck in Backward Talk

CHAPTER 1

When Talking Becomes Pointless

"Day by day nothing changes, but when you look back everything is different."

—C. S. Lewis

Sarah stared at her computer screen, her cursor blinking at the end of an unsent email. As VP of Product at TechFlow, she knew her top project was veering off course. The signs were everywhere: missed deadlines, growing tension between engineering and design, and a persistent undercurrent of frustration in team meetings.

The email she couldn't bring herself to send was to Marco, her star engineer, and to Michelle, the design lead. She wanted them to hash out the conflicting priorities together. Marco was focused on performance and scalability. Michelle wanted a more modern, surprising user experience. Both were doing excellent work but pursuing different goals.

Sarah had drafted the message three times. Each version sounded too confrontational. What if it turned into a blame session? What if she made things worse?

"I'll wait until after the board presentation," she thought, closing the draft. "I don't want this to become a distraction when we need to show progress." She convinced herself that things might settle on their own.

They didn't.

Two months later, she sat in her office, holding Marco's resignation letter in complete shock.

I've accepted an offer elsewhere, it read. *I need an environment where I can make a real impact.*

The exit interview confirmed her worst fear: Marco had felt caught between impossible priorities, unsure which direction the team wanted to go. He wasn't getting the clarity he needed and felt increasingly isolated.

The irony was crushing. Sarah had avoided the conversation with Marco to protect her board presentation. Instead, she found herself explaining to the board why her star engineer had quit.

Had they spoken earlier, establishing clarity and intent, the project might still be on track. Marco might still be on the team. And he might even have helped bridge the gap with design.

Sadly, Sarah's story isn't unique. It plays out daily in organizations worldwide.

Conversations can make or break results—their power cannot be overstated. When teams engage in meaningful dialogue, they can overcome any obstacle, but when conversations go wrong (or, worse, never happen at all), teams end up stuck in cycles of blame, regret, and "what-if" scenarios that lead nowhere.

And the cost can be staggering.

The Conversation That Never Happened—a $359 Billion Crisis

When teams fail, the root cause isn't always what we think. We blame deadlines, budgets, bad hires, or market conditions. But beneath the surface, there's often something simpler, and more fixable: the conversation that never happens.

Small problems quietly grow into major problems—not because no one sees them coming, but because no one dared to speak up.

Talented people leave—not because they can't do the job, but because they never get the clarity or support they need to succeed.

The numbers reveal the true cost of avoidance. Instead of addressing issues directly, professionals fall into familiar, costly patterns. A study by Crucial Learning shows that 43 percent of respondents spend two weeks or more every year ruminating about unresolved problems at work.[2] And yet, instead of speaking up, they resort to a host of harmful, resource-sapping behaviors, including:

- complaining to others (77 percent)
- doing extra or unnecessary work (63 percent)
- ruminating about the problem (57 percent)
- getting angry (49 percent)

Each day, as crucial conversations go unspoken, opportunities for early intervention slip away. The cost extends far beyond individual projects. According to a study by CPP (publisher of the Myers-Briggs assessment), US employees spend an average of 2.8 hours per week dealing with conflict, costing businesses an estimated $359 billion annually in lost productivity.[3]

But those statistics don't show the whole picture. The real tragedy isn't just the financial cost—it's the human cost. Talented team members like Marco leave. Innovation stagnates. Trust erodes. Teams that should be creating value instead create frustration.

So, the question isn't whether these conversations matter. It's this: Why do even the smartest, most capable professionals consistently struggle to have them?

We've Been Chasing the Wrong Problem

For decades, the conventional wisdom has been clear: People avoid difficult conversations because they're afraid. They have a fear of conflict, a fear of damaging relationships, a fear of retaliation, or even a fear of rejection.

This explanation seems intuitively correct, since we've all experienced the physical symptoms that accompany a high-stakes conversation—the racing heart, the shallow breath, and the mental spiral of worst-case scenarios. Our bodies react as if we're preparing for danger, because on some level, we are.

The fix seems equally clear: Focus on the environment. If fear is a natural reaction to uncertainty about how others might respond, then we need to reduce the fear. However, while fear is automatic, silence is a choice.

So naturally, the solution has focused on making the conversational setting safer and more comfortable: Create psychological safety. Reduce conflict. Build trust first, then tackle difficult topics.

But what if this explanation is incomplete—or even fundamentally wrong?

When Speaking Up Becomes Pointless

My research with 5,350 professionals across multiple industries revealed something that changes everything we thought we knew about workplace communication.

At first, the pattern seemed familiar. When I asked individuals why *other people* avoid difficult conversations, 73.5 percent of respondents cited "fear of conflict" as the primary reason. It's the same old explanation we've heard for years.

When I asked people why *they personally* avoid these conversations, however, the results were strikingly different:

Only 30 percent cited fear as their reason for staying silent.

Instead, the most common reason—shared by 64.6 percent—was something else entirely: **"It won't change anything."**

This disconnect reveals what I call the "Pointlessness Paradox": We assume that fear drives other people, while we find ourselves driven by an internal sense of futility. We don't avoid conversations because we're scared to speak—we avoid them because we believe speaking up is useless.

Consider this testimony from a senior manager in my study: "After raising concerns three times with no response, I learned that speaking up was pointless. It wasn't that I was afraid to share my concerns—I didn't want to waste my time and social capital on something that wouldn't change anyway."

That shift—from courage to resignation—is what the Pointlessness Paradox is really about.

Think about your own experience. How many times have you stayed silent, not because you were afraid of the conversation, but because you doubted it would even matter? How often have you seen colleagues raise important issues, only to watch their concerns disappear into a void of inaction?

Why Smart People Give Up

This Pointlessness Paradox describes patterns that the fear-based model never could.

Why do confident senior leaders often stay silent about strategic concerns?

Why do experienced professionals withhold valuable insights during critical decisions?

Why do teams with excellent interpersonal relationships still struggle with crucial conversations?

It's because many of them have learned—often the hard way—that speaking up doesn't lead to change.

But there's more to it than just disappointing experiences.

Most professionals have never been trained in the art of difficult conversations. Worse, many were actually taught by their own leaders *not* to have them. They learned to "manage up," to "pick their battles," and to wait for the "right time," which often never comes. The unspoken rule is clear: Pushing back can be risky, even disloyal.

Over time, this becomes a pattern:

- You raise a strategy concern. It's acknowledged but never acted on.

- You suggest a process improvement. Everyone agrees, but nothing changes.
- You flag a risk. People nod, but no one follows up.

Each non-response teaches the same lesson: *Your voice doesn't matter here. Speaking up is a waste of political capital. Real decisions happen elsewhere, in conversations you're not a part of.*

This creates a vicious cycle: The less that people speak up, the more convinced they become that speaking up is pointless. Leaders often mistake silence for alignment, and issues go unaddressed until they escalate into crises. By the time problems are impossible to ignore, the team's capacity for honest dialogue has already eroded.

The Pointlessness Paradox explains why traditional solutions often fail. Creating psychological safety addresses fear, but it doesn't address futility. Making conversations more comfortable is helpful, but it doesn't make them more impactful. The result is teams working in "safe" environments, while simultaneously believing their voices don't matter.

Why Our Brains Work Against Us

The Pointlessness Paradox becomes even more powerful when we understand the science behind it. Evolutionarily, we're wired to treat social risk like physical danger, which helps explain why difficult conversations feel more than just uncomfortable.

Social threats feel like physical threats. Research from the NeuroLeadership Institute shows that when we anticipate difficult conversations, our brains activate the same threat-detection systems designed to protect us from predators.[4] The amygdala hijacks logical thinking, blood flow redirects to emotional processing, and we lose access to the precise skills needed for effective dialogue.

This biological response made perfect sense in a time when social rejection could mean literal death through exclusion from the tribe. In modern organizations, however, this same defense mechanism often causes more harm than good. The stress response doesn't just make us avoid conversations—it makes us terrible at having them, reinforcing our belief that they're pointless.

We overestimate our courage. In a study by VitalSmarts, 95 percent of participants confidently claimed they would confront someone cutting in line.[5] Yet when it actually happened, only one in fifteen spoke up. The rest said nothing, venting their anger afterward.

This gap between intention and action shows up in high-stakes environments, too. Research from healthcare settings reveals that 90 percent of nurses won't speak up to a doctor even when patient safety is at risk.[6] Similarly, 93 percent of workers who spot potential accidents stay silent even when colleagues could be harmed.[7]

We consistently overestimate our willingness to speak up when it matters most. But when reality hits and we don't say something, it reinforces the narrative that we're not equipped for these conversations—that they truly are pointless for people like us.

Avoidance becomes self-reinforcing. Every time we postpone tough conversations, we reinforce a feedback loop that makes future discussions harder. Silence does provide short-term relief—similar to the temporary satisfaction of avoiding a challenging workout. But just like skipping exercise, that temporary comfort ultimately leads to long-term weakness.

Issues don't disappear when ignored; they compound. What starts as a minor annoyance—perhaps a colleague who frequently interrupts—morphs into a bigger problem. We begin seeing them not just as someone who interrupted us once, but as "an interrupter." That becomes their identity in our eyes. Over time, we dread working with that colleague entirely, confirming our belief that the relationship is beyond repair.

And that's just one example. These small moments of avoidance don't stay small—they accumulate.

Silence Is Not Cheap

This gradual buildup is what I call "conversational debt"—the growing cost of all the crucial conversations we avoid or mismanage. Much like financial debt, conversational debt starts small and compounds over time, resulting in exponentially greater costs than the original discomfort we sought to avoid.

At first, it seems manageable and harmless: a concern left unspoken here, a decision rushed there, and a conflict smoothed over rather than addressed.

But the compound interest quickly grows out of control as small issues become significant problems. Minor tensions escalate into departmental conflicts, and strategic misalignments evolve into organizational crises. Every conversation we avoid makes the next one more challenging to have, and every issue we defer becomes more complex to resolve. Every act of silence teaches others that speaking up isn't welcome.

The irony is painful: In trying to protect ourselves and others from discomfort, we create the conditions for much greater pain.

The conversation that Sarah avoided with Marco cost them both far more than any awkward feedback session ever could have.

Teams that understand this principle make a different choice: They recognize that avoiding difficult conversations costs more than having them. They develop the capability to address issues before they compound into crises.

Moving Forward

The journey from avoidance to action begins with acknowledging a simple truth: The conversations we're not (really) having are costing us more than we think.

Conversations don't just go wrong when they're avoided, but when they fail to address the real issues. When we play nice, dance around conflict, or settle for vague agreement, that, too, is a form of avoidance, with consequences just as damaging. This more subtle form of avoidance explains why traditional approaches—like "just speak up" or "be more direct"—so often fail.

The good news? These patterns also point the way forward. By recognizing how personal fears, team dynamics, and organizational culture interact, we can begin to create environments where crucial conversations become possible, even natural. This understanding sets the stage for Forward Talk, a practical approach for transforming how teams communicate, which we'll explore in the next chapter.

CHAPTER 2

The Forward Talk Model

"All problems exist in the absence of a good conversation."

—Thomas Leonard

At twenty-three, just three weeks into my new role as VP of Strategy at a global advertising agency, I found myself in a client presentation that would forever change my understanding of conversations.

Growing up playing rugby taught me something essential: When a teammate is getting unfairly hammered, you don't just watch from the sidelines. You step in.

We were presenting three campaign concepts to a client. The CEO immediately picked his favorite—the safe, conventional approach. Everyone nodded in unison.

Everyone except Zora, a junior marketing associate who raised her hand. "That one's too cliché. It won't help us stand out against the competition. Option B felt more unique and on-brand."

The room went ice-cold.

"That's the stupidest idea I've heard all week," the CEO erupted. His tone turned vicious, condescending. "Maybe you should leave these decisions to people with experience."

He dismissed her with a wave and continued his attack for another excruciating minute.

The room froze. My boss studied his notes. My colleagues found their shoes fascinating. No one said a thing.

In the hushed room, I spoke up. "Actually, I think Zora's right," I said. "You'd be missing a real opportunity if you didn't explore it further. And that's not how you treat people."

Dead silence. Everyone stared at me as if I'd committed career suicide. The CEO turned red.

"Who the hell are you to tell me how to treat my employees?!"

The meeting ended abruptly. I walked out, certain I'd been fired.

But soon, something shifted. Over the following weeks, the CEO's tone began to change. While he had a reputation for dismissing feedback and making people feel foolish for challenging him, he started treating his team with more respect and became more open to dissenting views. And eventually, he did give campaign B a chance, and it succeeded brilliantly, proof that challenging assumptions can lead to great results.

The lesson was simple: Sometimes you must speak up, even when it feels pointless—or even if you're scared. The conversations we tend to avoid are often the ones that can change everything.

What Is Forward Talk?

"Forward Talk" is simple but powerful. It's the discipline of having conversations that accomplish two things:

1. **Address the real issue:** It tackles the root cause, not the symptoms, excuses, or side topics.
2. **Focus on the future:** It's about what needs to happen next—finding a resolution—rather than dwelling on what went wrong in the past.

That's the formula: **Address the real issue + focus on the future.**

Forward Talk is the antidote to the three patterns that keep teams stuck—avoidance, blame, and groupthink—and will fundamentally change how you handle team conversations. Forward Talk builds both individual and team capacity to transform everyday discussions into drivers of progress, not just moments of comfort.

I call it *Forward Talk* because it moves you *forward*—toward understanding, resolution, and real commitment—and because *talk* is casual, human, and action-oriented.

This isn't a theoretical model filled with rigid scripts or step-by-step solutions. Instead, Forward Talk is an actionable framework to elevate the quality of your team conversations.

Conversations are the foundation of collaboration.[8] When done right, they move teams forward. When done wrong—or avoided entirely—they become the invisible forces that keep talented teams from reaching their potential.

Forward Talk goes beyond managing conflict. It applies to high-stakes decisions, brainstorming sessions, feedback discussions, and even Zoom calls. The quality of those talks determines whether your team improves or remains stuck.

From Pointlessness to Possibility

As Brené Brown explains in *The Gifts of Imperfection*, hope isn't an emotion.[9] Rather, it's a capability we build through adversity and trusted relationships. That moment when I stood up to the CEO taught me something else profound: Hope is a capability you build.

I want you and your team to regain not just conversational skills, but hope—hope that speaking up matters, that conversations can lead to change, and that progress is possible. Not hope masquerading as naive optimism or wishful thinking, but hope grounded in capability.

Here's what I've learned working with hundreds of teams worldwide: Instead of waiting for perfect conditions or hoping for the other person to be "open to feedback," you must develop the skills to navigate these conversations systematically. Forward Talk provides you with frameworks that work, tools that reduce guesswork, and practices that build your conversational muscle.

Even if it requires that you go first.

Hope builds confidence, and confidence in turn increases hope. Each conversation becomes practice. When you turn a difficult conversation into a productive outcome, your confidence grows. Conversation after conversation, you realize your voice matters, making you feel more hopeful.

Forward Talk helps your team move:

- from apathy to participation
- from avoidance to addressing tensions
- from symptoms to root causes
- from blame to problem-solving
- from superficial alignment to real commitment

If you're reading this thinking, *Yes, but my team is different*, you're not alone. I've heard that before, too. And I've seen "hopeless" teams make real progress.

The discomfort of speaking up never completely disappears—and that's okay. However, building your capacity for hope will help you move through that discomfort with purpose.

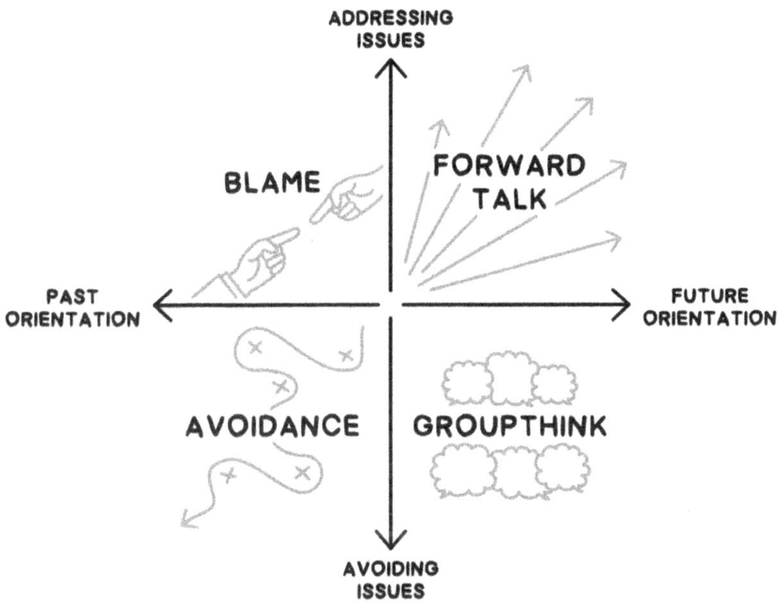

The Forward Talk Framework

Your team faces a paradox: You need better conversations more than ever, but the way you currently talk might be making things worse.

Instead of clarity, you get confusion. Instead of momentum, you get avoidance, blame, and groupthink.

To fix this, the Forward Talk framework is built on two essential dimensions:

- **Time Orientation:** Are conversations stuck in the past or focused on the future?
- **Issue Engagement:** Are people avoiding the real issue or addressing it head-on?

These two axes create four zones, only one of which leads to meaningful action: Forward Talk.

The Three Patterns That Derail Teams

To use Forward Talk effectively, we first need to understand the three Backward Talk traps that prevent teams from having meaningful conversations.

The first and most common trap is simple **avoidance**.

Avoidance results from thinking that conversations are pointless, but it's also the product of people not caring about improving things. Some stop caring over time, while others may never have felt invested enough to engage deeply in the first place. Teams remain focused on past results and outcomes.

When teams fall into this pattern, they may recognize issues but choose not to address them, hoping they'll resolve themselves or fearing the consequences of speaking up. This silence comes at a cost—problems persist, trust erodes, and the team's ability to tackle challenges diminishes over time. The temporary comfort of avoidance gives way to a persistent undercurrent of frustration and disengagement.

The second pattern emerges when teams do address issues, but they get trapped in the **blame** game.

These conversations focus on team members finding fault with others and defending their own positions rather than solving problems. While it may feel like issues are being addressed when individuals speak up, blame instead gets us stuck in the past, creating defensiveness and eroding trust. Teams caught in this pattern may have lots of "honest conversations" that leave everyone feeling worse and resolve nothing.

The third pattern is perhaps the most insidious: **groupthink**.

Here, teams maintain a facade of harmony by avoiding real engagement with issues. They may talk about moving forward and staying positive, but without addressing underlying tensions, this creates only superficial alignment at best. Important perspectives remain unvoiced, and real problems continue unchallenged beneath the illusion of agreement.

Avoidance, blame, and groupthink are the enemies of collaboration—they damage your team's conversations.

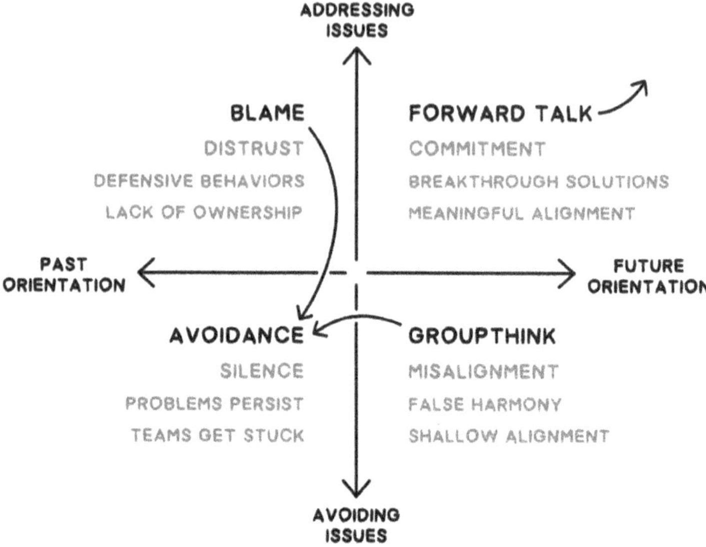

Here's how the three backward patterns reinforce each other:

Blame creates *distrust.* When conversations focus on finding fault, people become defensive and stop taking ownership. Teams may address issues, but relationships fracture.

Groupthink causes *misalignment.* When everyone agrees too fast to preserve harmony, it feels like progress. But shallow alignment often breaks down—soon, teams realize they never really were on the same page.

Avoidance leads to *silence*—both as a pattern and as a consequence. When people are afraid of being blamed or feel like their voice doesn't matter, they stop speaking up. Problems persist and teams get stuck in vicious cycles.

Forward Talk builds *commitment*—it's the only way to make real progress. When teams address real problems and focus on solutions, they create breakthrough ideas and true alignment.

What's fascinating is how these Backward Talk patterns become self-reinforcing, and that is exactly what makes them so dangerous. One CTO I worked with described it perfectly: "We stopped having real conversations because they always ended badly, but they ended badly because we'd stopped having real conversations."

Avoidance leads to bigger problems that become even harder to discuss. Blame creates defensive behaviors that trigger more blame. And groupthink gradually diminishes the team's ability to even recognize issues that need addressing.[10] Over time, these patterns become part of the culture—"how we do things here"—the team's default way of handling (or not handling) difficult situations.

But I've also seen the transformative power of Forward Talk in action.

One of the most striking examples came from a healthcare leadership team facing serious patient safety issues. At first, they were stuck in a cycle of blame—their conversations centered on finding a scapegoat. When incidents occurred, meetings became forensic exercises: Who missed the warning signs? Which department dropped the ball? Who should have escalated faster?

The finger-pointing was destroying morale. Nurses stopped reporting near-misses for fear of being blamed. Doctors became defensive about protocols. Everyone protected themselves instead of patients.

Over time they learned to shift the conversation. Instead of asking "Whose fault was this?," they asked, "What in our system allowed this to happen?" Instead of dissecting past failures, they focused on preventing future ones. They replaced their usual pattern of blame and defensiveness with a future-focused and solution-oriented one.

The difference was remarkable. The same people who had been afraid to speak up were now actively engaged in finding solutions.

Forward Talk breaks these destructive cycles by changing both what teams talk about and how they do it. Your team needs both the courage to address real issues and the discipline to focus on the future. Together, these bring the hope of resolution.

Forward Talk vs. Backward Talk

To create lasting change in how teams communicate, we first need to understand what distinguishes Forward Talk from Backward Talk.

The table below highlights six dimensions of how Forward Talk can transform the way your team communicates. Use them as a lens to reflect on your team's current habits—and where there's room to grow.

Think of a recent team meeting. Did your team's conversations resemble the patterns of Backward Talk or the qualities of Forward Talk?

Dimension	Backward Talk	Forward Talk
Time Orientation	Past-anchored	Future-focused
Focus	Avoiding or blaming	Addressing directly
Energy	Depleting	Energizing
Style	Defensive & fear-driven	Generative & courage-based
Depth	Surface-level fixes	Root cause understanding
Result	**Getting stuck—or moving backward**	**Resolving issues—and committing to action**

The best way to understand how these patterns work is to observe them in action. Forward Talk helps you reframe conversations when you notice that discussions are going backward: When teams try to table discussions indefinitely, you instead ask what can be decided now. When they dwell on shifting priorities, you focus on the lessons already learned. When everyone agrees too quickly, you surface the unspoken concerns.

The following examples show how to move from Backward Talk to Forward Talk:

Backward Talk	→	Forward Talk
"Our manager is not here. Let's table this until our next meeting."		"What decision can we make with the authority we have?"
"The other departments never communicate properly."		"How can we clarify our expectations so we get the information we need?"
"Everyone seems OK with this approach. We're aligned."		"Before we commit, what concerns haven't we surfaced yet?"

But what actually drives productive, Forward Talk–style conversations? When things go right, what's happening beneath the surface?

The Drivers of Productive Conversations

We often assume productive conversations are smooth, agreeable, and free of friction. But in reality, progress comes from dialogue that's honest, sometimes uncomfortable, and grounded in mutual respect. So, what actually drives a conversation forward, especially when the stakes are high or views differ?

My research identified three key drivers of productive conversations:

- openness despite disagreement (83 percent of respondents)
- feeling heard (79 percent)
- clarity on next steps (71 percent)

Yet in order for these drivers to surface, some original discomfort is required: voicing disagreement, conveying your feeling of not being heard, or having the courage to ask for clarity. Notice what's missing? "Everyone agrees." "There's no tension." "It went smoothly."

Forward Talk isn't always comfortable. Real conversations are often messy. They're characterized by honest engagement, attentive listening, and clear direction, regardless of whether everyone agrees.

This finding fundamentally challenges how most organizations approach team communication. We don't need to create artificial consensus or suppress disagreement to move forward. In fact, multiple studies,[11] not just mine, confirm that the absence of conflict doesn't signal agreement—it often signals apathy. When people stop disagreeing, it tends to be because they've already stopped caring.

Recognizing Backward Talk Patterns

Before we can shift how we communicate, we need to understand the habits holding us back. These often manifest in subtle, everyday ways that go unnoticed—until they begin to affect performance and trust. Take a moment to consider these questions about your team's dynamics:

Do people preface their ideas with defensive statements like "I know this might sound crazy, but . . . "?	☐ Yes ☐ No
Does your team spend more time discussing who's responsible than how to move forward?	☐ Yes ☐ No
Do team members often withhold their real concerns until after decisions are final?	☐ Yes ☐ No
Has your team stopped experimenting because "we tried that before"?	☐ Yes ☐ No
Does the energy noticeably drain during important discussions?	☐ Yes ☐ No

If you answered "yes" to two or more of these questions, your team may be caught in Backward Talk patterns. But don't worry—you're not alone. Most organizations get stuck in endless conversational loops without realizing it.

The good news is that there's a way forward, and the first step is recognizing the early signs of avoidance, blame, and groupthink. Once you shift from Backward Talk to Forward Talk, you'll be able to drive more productive conversations.

In the next chapter, we'll examine conversational debt—the hidden cost teams incur by avoiding conversations. After all, issues don't go away when we ignore them. They compound.

CHAPTER 3

Conversational Debt

"A man in debt is so far a slave."

—Ralph Waldo Emerson

Crises don't come out of nowhere. When a CEO tells me, "We never saw it coming," I know I'll find a trail of warnings that were ignored, or dozens of important conversations that never happened.

This is exactly what I discovered at a global pharmaceutical company that brought me in after their most promising drug development project got stuck. Dr. Ewa, the lead scientist, had been warning about trial results for months. Each time, the global project director dismissed her: "We'll address that once we get closer to FDA approval."

But Dr. Ewa had twenty years of experience in drug development. She knew FDA approval was serious business. The first time the director brushed her off, she gave him the kind of look you reserve for someone trying to sell you a bridge. The second time, she laughed at how ridiculous it was for him to ignore her. By the third time, she'd stopped trying altogether.

The rest of the team? They said nothing. They were taking notes, as if that would change anything. No one wanted to get caught in the crossfire.

Rather than listening to Dr. Ewa, the director only wanted to share good news with the CEO. Data analysis could wait. His relentless push for progress created a "positivity" culture where problems were seen as roadblocks, rather than insight.

By the time I was brought in, the damage was almost irreversible. The project needed a reset because of the exact data inconsistencies that Dr. Ewa had been flagging all along.

What I found most troubling wasn't the missed opportunity—it was how predictable the failure had been. Everyone saw the warning signs, but the necessary conversations never happened. This is what I call "conversational debt," and its cost can be crushing.

Silence Has a Hefty Price Tag

Think about that parking ticket you kept meaning to pay, telling yourself you'd handle it next week. By the time you remembered, the $50 fine had become $150 with late fees and administrative charges. What started as a minor expense had tripled while sitting in your drawer.

Teams accumulate a similar burden—one that compounds not in dollars, but in lost trust and missed opportunities.

Conversational debt refers to the accumulating cost of the crucial conversations that we handle poorly or avoid altogether. Like financial debt, it compounds over time, making it almost impossible to address.

The mathematics of silence is brutal. Every avoided conversation makes the next one more challenging to have. Every issue deferred becomes more complex to resolve. Every tension that goes unaddressed grows stronger and more expensive to fix.

Consider how conversational debt accumulates, from its initial balance all the way through the final collection notice:

- **Initial Balance:** A team member has concerns about a project timeline but stays silent to avoid being seen as negative.
- **Interest Accrual:** The unrealistic timeline creates stress, rushed work, and quality issues. Other team members notice the disturbance, but also stay quiet, adding their own concerns to the debt pile.
- **Compound Effect:** Mounting pressure leads to missed deadlines, frustrated stakeholders, and blame-shifting. The original timing concern evolves into a trust crisis, a quality issue, and a problem of team morale.
- **Collection Time:** By the time the debt comes due—usually in the form of project failure, key departures, or client complaints—the simple conversation that could have prevented everything now requires organizational crisis management.

As we saw with the pharmaceutical team, a conversation that didn't happen—a straightforward conversation about trial data concerns—compounded into strategic failure, relationship damage, and millions in lost investments.

The Hidden Tax on High Performance

Few workplace challenges are as costly—or as overlooked—as conversational debt. While most organizations feel the strain of miscommunication, few stop to calculate its cumulative impact or recognize its root causes. Yet the signs are everywhere.

My research revealed the true symptoms of teams suffering from conversational debt:

- The same issues surface repeatedly (82.1 percent of respondents).
- Meetings end without real decisions or outcomes (72.1 percent).
- Tensions escalate, but no resolution is reached (71.6 percent).
- People stay silent about what they really think (71.2 percent).

These aren't dramatic blowups or heated arguments. Rather, they're the quiet signs of a team slowly drowning in unspoken concerns, unresolved tensions, and unaddressed misalignments.

The signs of conversational debt are subtle but easy to observe:

- People agree too quickly to avoid being labeled as "difficult."
- The real conversations often occur in the hallway, after the meeting ends.
- Teams schedule yet another "follow-up meeting" because decisions are never final.
- Zoom calls feel tense, but no one mentions it.
- The same questions keep surfacing in every all-hands meeting.

The research reveals a devastating paradox: The conversations that teams avoid are precisely the ones that end up destroying them. Teams face a binary choice—whether to pay the modest cost of having difficult conversations today or to endure the crushing expense of accumulated silence tomorrow.

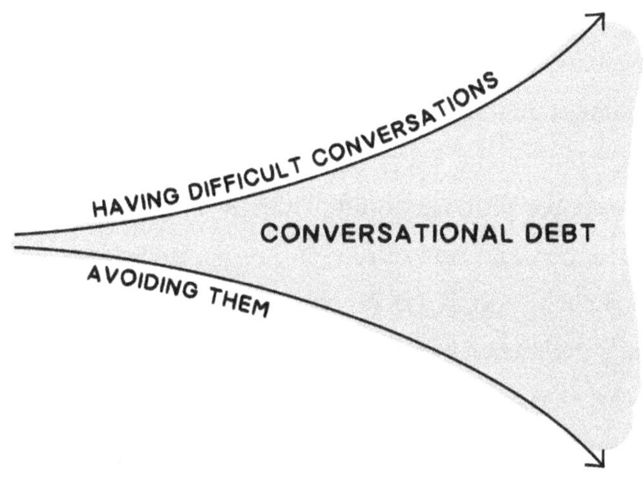

The Three Types of Debt

Conversational debt accumulates in three distinct but interconnected ways. Like a financial portfolio gone awry, issues in one area can exacerbate problems in others. While some teams carry a heavier load in one category, most are juggling all three debts simultaneously.

These three types of conversational debt connect to the ABCs of culture:[12] Alignment, Belonging, and Collaboration. I've used this framework for over ten years to help teams build healthier cultures. Every successful team needs all three parts working together.

Alignment is about having a shared future; it gives direction on where we're headed. *Belonging* is the glue that binds people together; it makes a group of people feel like one. *Collaboration* is how work gets done; it transforms words into action.

When teams avoid these conversations or handle them poorly, the culture breaks down. That's exactly how conversational debt forms and why it's so damaging.

Alignment debt occurs when teams confuse nodding heads with genuine commitment. Everyone appears to agree in meetings, but people leave with fundamentally different interpretations of decisions, priorities, and next steps.

I've watched leadership teams commit to "rapid scaling" only to discover, months later, that each executive had completely different ideas about what that meant. The CTO focused on new technologies, the CFO maintained restrictive approval processes, and the CSO continued to push legacy products. Everyone thought they were supporting the strategy.

Belonging debt accumulates when teams prioritize artificial harmony over authentic dialogue. People withhold concerns, soften feedback, and avoid challenging popular ideas to maintain group cohesion.

At one creative agency, a star team presented work that was completely off-brief. However, because the team was so beloved and award-winning, everyone gave polite, surface-level feedback. Yet the client (predictably) rejected the campaign, deeming it "totally irrelevant," which ultimately cost the agency the account.

Collaboration debt builds when teams fail to reach a resolution. Decisions are never final, meetings end by scheduling another meeting, and simple disagreements transform into endless discussions. Teams get stuck debating who has authority, while the opportunities to make important decisions slip away.

I've seen cross-functional teams spend weeks discussing product features without anyone clarifying who is actually responsible for making the final call.

The Debt Spiral

The three types of conversational debt don't exist in isolation, but feed one another in a dangerous spiral. Poor alignment leads to misunderstandings and harms relationships, making collaboration harder. Weak collaboration then prevents teams from surfacing and resolving misalignments. As their sense of belonging deteriorates, trust disappears, and team members stop being honest altogether.

I watched this unfold at a software company, where minor differences in the interpretation of their agile methodology (**alignment debt**) led developers to hesitate in raising concerns about sprint planning (**belonging debt**). This hesitation resulted in poor cross-team coordination (**collaboration debt**), which further confused their understanding of the methodology.

The spiral accelerated: As misunderstandings accumulated, engineers stopped flagging issues during retrospectives, fearing they'd be seen as difficult. One team delayed raising a blocker that affected another team's deployment, and by the time it surfaced, the release had to be rolled back, costing the company two weeks of work.

Eventually, most sprint meetings were spent managing the fallout from previous sprints. People tiptoed around recurring problems, focusing on what had gone wrong instead of how to move forward.

Rather than recalibrating the team's understanding of "rapid scaling," conversations circled back to blame and rework. Conversational debt had overtaken the team's ability to function.

Breaking the Debt Spiral Cycle

The path forward begins with recognition. Your team must acknowledge its conversational debt and understand how it manifests across the three dimensions.

However, recognition alone isn't enough. To successfully repair this debt, teams must progress from avoidance to genuine commitment—the Forward Talk journey. Understanding that journey, which we'll discuss further in the next chapter, helps you see where your team currently operates and what's required to move forward.

The Natural Progression Forward

Most teams don't transform their conversations overnight. They progress through natural stages, each addressing a distinct type of debt.

The first breakthrough occurs when someone finally breaks the silence, naming the issue that everyone has been avoiding. This single act creates space for authentic participation, legitimizing any necessary conversations and directly addressing the belonging debt that keeps people withdrawn.

Once the silence is broken, multiple perspectives begin to emerge as people feel safer sharing their real thoughts. Teams may discover they've been making completely different assumptions about the same issues. This stage addresses both belonging and alignment debt—as diverse viewpoints surface, teams realize just how much they didn't know about everyone else's thinking.

The next progression involves moving beyond surface complaints to understanding deeper patterns. Instead of treating the symptoms, teams start examining the underlying system issues. This builds capacity for productive tension and breaks the superficial problem-solving patterns that characterize collaboration debt.

As teams become more comfortable with authentic dialogue, their energy shifts from problem-focused to solution-focused. They develop shared ownership of the path forward through collaborative exploration.

Ultimately, their dialogue evolves into concrete commitments with clear accountability, demonstrating that speaking up leads to tangible change rather than endless discussion.

Where Teams Get Stuck

Most teams get stuck at the first stage—they see the issues but can't break through the silence barrier. Others reach the second stage but retreat to artificial harmony when tensions rise. The most successful teams learn to navigate fluidly through this progression, treating authentic dialogue as natural rather than exceptional.

The journey becomes self-reinforcing, as each successful navigation builds the team's capacity to handle more complex conversations and prevents debt from reaccumulating in the future.

But navigating this progression doesn't happen by chance—it requires a shared language, consistent practice, and actionable tools. That's where the Forward Talk process comes in.

CHAPTER 4

From Avoidance to Commitment

"Action cures fear. Inaction creates terror."

—Douglas Horton

Teams handle difficult conversations in remarkably different ways. In my Culture Design Masterclass,[13] I ask participants about the best and worst cultures they've ever experienced. Their answers reflect how teams struggle with difficult conversations.

Pete, a creative director in one of my sessions, shared a story about two agencies that captures both extremes perfectly.

At CreativeCore, critical campaign discussions were avoided through deflection. "We'll sort that out later" and "Let's not overcomplicate things" were common mantras. When team members raised concerns, they were brushed off with "That's not the creative vision" or "Just trust us." Pete saw that though everyone nodded in meetings, their body language told the real story. Creative reviews ended with everyone appearing aligned, but that harmony vanished the moment they were in front of the client.

At InnovateAgency, the campaign meetings were completely different. When reviewing concepts, the executive creative director deliberately invited the account and strategy teams to find potential problems. "What client pushback are we not seeing? Where could this fail?" Pete watched as teams actively looked for issues before they became real problems. There was tension—real tension—but people stayed engaged and respectful. After meetings, everyone was truly committed to making the campaign succeed because they felt heard and valued.

"The funny thing," Pete told the group, "is that CreativeCore meetings seemed smoother and more polite. Everyone appeared to agree, but nobody had ownership. At InnovateAgency, meetings were messier and sometimes uncomfortable, but we solved problems right away and everyone wanted the campaigns to succeed."

Unlike CreativeCore, InnovateAgency knew how to turn feedback into investment—moving from surface-level alignment to genuine commitment.

Same kinds of people. Same kinds of challenges. Completely different outcomes.

The Avoidance Trap

When teams address only superficial issues or avoid conversations completely, they get stuck in Backward Talk loops.

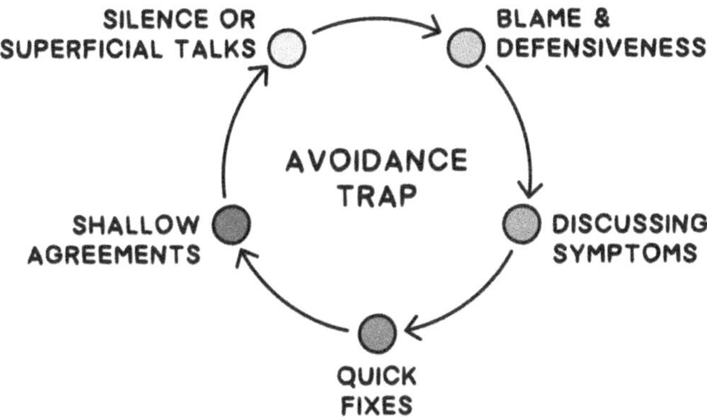

These destructive patterns show how avoidance compounds problems over time. Each Backward Talk loop deepens the conversational debt and makes recovery even more challenging.

The Avoidance Trap represents the worst state for team dynamics. It's the place where crucial conversations are deferred, tensions simmer beneath the surface, and artificial harmony masks deep misalignment.

But there's a way out.

The Forward Talk Journey: Five Milestones to Navigate Conversational Debt

Think of moving from avoidance to commitment as a journey rather than a checklist. You don't need to follow a rigid sequence—you can begin wherever you are and make progress from there.

These five milestones represent the key moments across team conversations. Some teams excel at generating solutions but struggle to initiate difficult talks. Others are great at surfacing issues but get stuck in the analysis. But remember the goal isn't to rush from one milestone to the next—that's exactly the problem with teams that rush into action without addressing the real issues.

FORWARD TALK: FIVE-MILESTONE JOURNEY

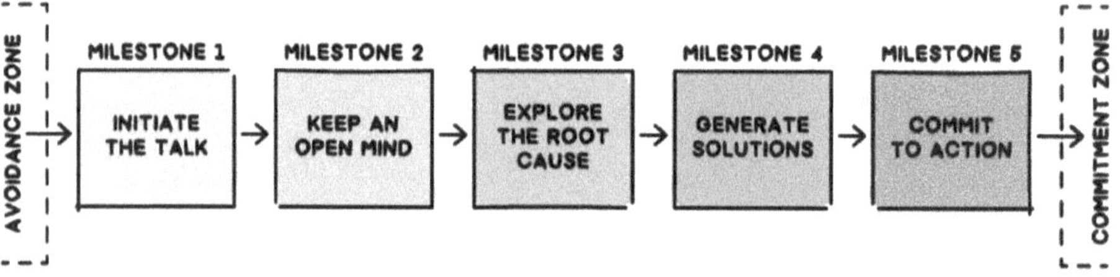

Milestone 1: Initiate the Talk

Backward Talk pattern: Your team knows that something needs discussing, but no one wants to go first.

What a solution can look like: During a project planning meeting, I watched a team member handle an aggressive timeline brilliantly. Instead of complaining about the deadline, she said, "Given our current workload, if we commit to this timeline, we'll probably need to deprioritize some other work. What should we consider moving?"

By framing it as a capacity trade-off rather than a complaint, she made the real constraints visible without seeming difficult. More importantly, she invited the group to collaborate on prioritization rather than just voicing her concern—which immediately prompted others to start talking about what was realistic.

How this reduces conversational debt: This milestone primarily addresses belonging debt. By legitimizing necessary conversations, you create space for authentic participation regardless of hierarchy or role.

Reflection questions:

- What conversation are we avoiding that could prevent future problems if we held it now?
- What's the real cost of ignoring this issue?
- Who else might be waiting for someone to speak first?

Milestone 2: Keep an Open Mind

Backward Talk pattern: The silence is broken, but people are still guarded and defensive, or rush to judgment.

What a solution can look like: I once worked with teams after a difficult merger. One company kept saying, "We did better when we were independent," while the acquirer complained that people weren't accepting the new rules. Instead of letting them argue over exactly what was wrong, I asked the acquired company to reflect on how they'd improved since the merger. Then, I asked the acquirer to consider how the other company had made them better.

When both teams focused on finding the upside rather than defending their losses, they started seeing each other as complementary rather than adversarial.

How this reduces conversational debt: This milestone tackles both belonging and alignment debt. It allows diverse perspectives to emerge while starting the process of creating shared understanding.

Reflection questions:

- What truth do I need to share that I've been holding back?
- How open am I to having my views challenged?
- What if I'm the one who's wrong?

Milestone 3: Explore the Root Cause

Backward Talk pattern: You're discussing the issue, but conversations stay surface-level or keep circling back to the symptoms.

What a solution can look like: I once worked with a leadership team where people were spreading damaging rumors about the retiring leader's chosen successor. That same leader brought in HR and PR to not only stop the rumors but also identify who started them, which only made things worse.

When I facilitated sessions with senior executives, we discovered that the real issue wasn't the person—it was the process. People wanted a leader who represented the future, not someone handpicked to continue the same old approach. They were rejecting the leader's right to choose his own successor, not the successor himself.

How this reduces conversational debt: This milestone addresses collaboration debt. By moving beyond surface disagreements to understand underlying drivers, teams build the capacity for productive tension.

Reflection questions:

- What recurring patterns do I notice in our problems?
- What might others see that I'm missing?
- What questions haven't we asked yet?

Milestone 4: Generate Solutions

Backward Talk pattern: You understand the problem, but you're stuck in "we can't" thinking or defaulting to familiar solutions.

What a solution can look like: I once worked with leaders to debate remote work policies, trying to decide which roles should be in-person, remote, or hybrid based on job function. Instead of continuing the positional debate, someone suggested letting employees pitch their preferred arrangement and explain why it would work best.

The results surprised everyone: Young engineers lobbied for full office time because their home setups were terrible, while customer service staff members made compelling cases for hybrid work, showing how they could consolidate administrative tasks into specific days and work from home. This shift from assuming what each role needed to discovering what they wanted opened up solutions no one had considered.

How this reduces conversational debt: This milestone works on both collaboration and alignment debt. Through collaborative solution-finding, teams debate until they find the right approach, with the best idea winning.

Reflection questions:

- What solutions might emerge if we suspended all constraints?
- How could we approach this differently?
- What's the best idea, not the most popular?

Milestone 5: Commit to Action

Backward Talk pattern: You have good ideas and general agreement, but nothing concrete happens afterward.

What a solution can look like: I once worked with a team to finalize a major initiative where one member had serious doubts about the approach. Instead of fake agreement or continued resistance, she said, "I still have concerns about this direction, but I'm willing to commit fully. I suggest we tie everyone's quarterly bonus to this initiative's performance—including mine. If we're really doing this, we should all have skin in the game."

Her willingness to put her compensation at risk despite her doubts demonstrated genuine commitment rather than grudging compliance. It also challenged others to match that level of investment in making the decision work.

How this reduces conversational debt: This milestone integrates all three types of debt reduction. It creates clear alignment on the next steps, reinforces belonging through shared commitment, and enables future collaboration.

Reflection questions:

- What exactly are we committing to?
- What are we not aligned on?
- How can I put aside my differences and fully commit to this decision?

Starting Your Journey

The beauty of thinking about these milestones as a journey is that you can begin wherever your team needs the most help. Ask yourself: Where does our team typically get stuck? Do we avoid starting difficult conversations? Do we start them but become defensive? Do we explore issues but never find solutions? Do we generate ideas but never follow through?

Identify the issue, then start there. Master one milestone before worrying about the others. Each step you take builds your team's conversational muscle and eases the next part of the journey.

Can't wait to try this out now? The next chapter offers simple techniques for shifting conversations from Backward Talk to Forward Talk.

CHAPTER 5

Turn Backward Talk into Forward Talk

"A different language is a different vision of life."

—Federico Fellini

Now that you understand the five milestones for moving from avoidance to commitment, let's explore how you can redirect conversations when they get stuck.

Picture yourself in a meeting where colleagues dance around the real issue, rush to superficial agreement, or spiral into blame. You feel the energy draining, but how do you shift it?

When you notice a Backward Talk pattern, simply pause and reframe the conversation with a question that shifts the focus to Forward Talk.

The approach is straightforward: Don't fight the pattern or call it out—redirect it. Saying, "We shouldn't agree so quickly" shuts down dialogue, while asking "What concerns haven't we surfaced yet?" opens possibilities.

The goal is not to correct or confront others. Instead, you're offering a different lens. You're shifting the conversations from past-focused to future-focused, from symptoms to causes, from avoidance to engagement. The question itself does the work without creating resistance.

The power of these reframes is that they turn objections into possibilities. When someone says, "We need more data" or "That won't work," they're blocking dialogue. Instead, Forward Talk reframes these objections into questions that open new paths: "What do we know with the data we have?" or "What would happen if we tried this approach for a month?"

Reframing is how you begin with Forward Talk. As we continue through the book, we'll peel back additional layers, moving from these immediate interventions to addressing root causes, culture changes, and strategic solutions.

This chapter explains exactly how to make these interventions, featuring twenty-five conversational tools organized around the five milestones. You'll learn what to observe, when to step in, and how to effectively reframe the conversation.

FORWARD TALK: FIVE-MILESTONE JOURNEY

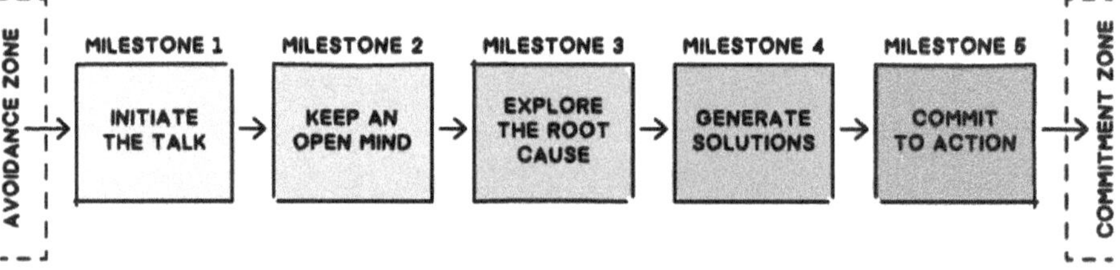

Milestone 1: Initiate the Talk

When teams recognize issues but can't seem to start difficult conversations, these reframes create safe entry points. Instead of forcing confrontation, they make the first step feel manageable and necessary.

Backward Talk: "We don't want to open that can of worms."
Forward Talk: "What's the cost of leaving this unresolved for another month?"

When teams avoid difficult topics, make the cost of silence explicit. Ask the team to estimate what happens if the issue remains unaddressed: Frustrated customers? Missed deadlines? Team stress? This reframes avoidance from "safe choice" to "expensive choice."

Backward Talk: "What's the point of speaking up? Nothing's going to change anyway."
Forward Talk: "What would prove that speaking up actually leads to action here?"

When teams sense futility, focus on demonstrable proof that input creates results. Ask: "If we made one decision right now based on what you're saying, what would that look like?" This tackles the core feeling of pointlessness that keeps people silent by creating immediate opportunities to prove that the system responds.

Backward Talk: "Let's table this until our next meeting."
Forward Talk: "What's the smallest piece of this that we could resolve right now?"

When teams want to defer everything, identify what micro-decision could be made immediately. Frame it as: "We can't redesign the whole process today, but could we agree on our criteria for a good solution?" This maintains momentum while respecting the issue's complexity.

Backward Talk: "If we ignore this, it'll probably go away on its own."
Forward Talk: "What happens if we wait another month to address this?"

When teams simply hope that problems will resolve themselves without intervention, force them to consider the compound cost of delay. Ask: "If we don't address this client's concern now, where will we be in four weeks?" This creates urgency by making clear that most problems get worse with time. Acting today is cheaper than managing crisis tomorrow.

Backward Talk: "The real conversation always happens after the meeting."
Forward Talk: "What is preventing us from having this conversation right now?"

When teams acknowledge the pattern of corridor conversations, address the barriers in real time. "If this is what people really think, why wait? What makes the hallway feel safer than this room?" This brings authentic dialogue into the formal meeting space.

Milestone 2: Keep an Open Mind

Once the conversation starts, teams often rush to judge or shut down perspectives that feel uncomfortable. The following reframes help slow things down and create space for diverse viewpoints.

Backward Talk: "Everyone seems comfortable with this approach."
Forward Talk: "Are we all comfortable or are we just not disagreeing out loud?"

When consensus feels too easy, directly challenge what the silence actually means. "I'm seeing a lot of nodding but not hearing any concerns. What's the difference between agreement and just not objecting?" This gives permission for people to voice any doubts they've been holding back.

Backward Talk: "I don't want to be the one to bring this up."
Forward Talk: "Who else is thinking what I'm thinking but not saying it?"

When someone hesitates to voice concerns, help them realize that they're probably not alone. "I'm sensing others might share this concern—who else is wondering about the timeline?" This reduces the isolation that keeps people silent, often revealing that individual doubts are actually shared team concerns.

Backward Talk: "Don't be so negative about this."
Forward Talk: "What valid concerns are being raised here?"

When someone gets labeled as negative for raising issues, redirect the focus to the concern itself. "Let's separate the message from the tone—what's the actual risk they're identifying?" This protects dissenting voices while staying focused on substance.

Backward Talk: "We all see this the same way."
Forward Talk: "What if we're completely wrong about what the real problem is?"

When teams assume they understand what's going on, challenge them. "Before we solve this, let's consider whether we've misdiagnosed what we're actually dealing with. What could we discover if we started from scratch?" This opens individuals to the possibility that the real issue might be completely different from what everyone assumes.

Backward Talk: "We don't want this to turn into a debate."
Forward Talk: "What would someone who disagrees with us completely say about this situation?"

When teams avoid productive conflict, prompt them to consider other perspectives. "If we brought in a consultant who thought we were totally wrong, what would they point out? How would they see this differently?" This helps teams escape their own echo chambers and consider radically different viewpoints.

Milestone 3: Explore the Root Cause

Teams often get stuck discussing symptoms rather than the underlying drivers. These reframes help conversations go deeper to address what's really causing problems.

Backward Talk: "We've tried this approach before and it didn't work."
Forward Talk: "What's different now that might make this approach work?"

When teams reject solutions based on past failures, explore what's changed. "When we tried this two years ago, we lacked budget and executive support. Do we have those now?" This prevents permanently ruling out good ideas based on outdated constraints.

Backward Talk: "We keep having the same problems over and over."
Forward Talk: "What pattern are we repeating, and how do we break it?"

When teams get frustrated with recurring issues, focus on pattern recognition and prevention. "If this keeps happening, what's the common thread? How do we break the cycle?" This transforms complaints into systematic learning.

Backward Talk: "Whose fault is this?"
Forward Talk: "Why does this same problem keep showing up in different forms?"

When blame starts, immediately redirect to the process rather than the person. Instead of moral explanations (character flaws), seek mechanical explanations (system gaps). Ask "What would prevent this pattern next time?" rather than "Who should have done what?"

Backward Talk: "Why didn't anyone speak up about this sooner?"
Forward Talk: "What makes problems like this hard to spot until they've gotten big?"

When teams blame people for not speaking up, examine what makes speaking up difficult. "What signals do we send about raising concerns? How could we encourage earlier feedback?" This shifts the focus from blaming silence to enabling voices.

Backward Talk: "We just need to fix this specific issue."
Forward Talk: "If this problem were a symptom, what would the disease be?"

When teams want to fix a symptom, use the medical metaphor to encourage systematic thinking. "Treating a fever doesn't cure the infection—what's the underlying condition creating this symptom? What would a doctor look for?" This helps teams move from reactive problem-solving to addressing the root causes.

Milestone 4: Generate Solutions

Once teams understand the real issues, they often get stuck in "we can't" thinking or default to safe solutions. These reframes open up creative problem-solving and fight groupthink.

Backward Talk: "That idea will never work here."
Forward Talk: "What would need to be true for this idea to succeed?"

When teams immediately dismiss suggestions, reframe the conversation to focus on conditions for success. "What would we have to change to make sure this idea works?" This moves from criticism to problem-solving while acknowledging real constraints.

Backward Talk: "We already have too much on our plate."
Forward Talk: "What can we pause or stop to make room for what matters most?"

When teams claim overload, force prioritization decisions. "If this is truly important, what becomes less important? What would we need to say no to?" This turns capacity constraints into strategic choices.

Backward Talk: "No, that won't work because . . . "
Forward Talk: "How might we build on it to make it work?"

Both "No, because . . . " and "Yes, but . . . " block creative thinking. The first dismisses ideas outright, while the second seems supportive despite immediately focusing on obstacles (passive-aggressive blocking). Use a "Yes, and . . . " approach to explore possibilities to grow the idea instead of killing it. Try "How might we modify that approach?" or "What if we combined that with . . . ?"

Backward Talk: "Let's stick to what we know works."
Forward Talk: "What's one bold move we haven't tried yet?"

When teams play it safe, challenge them to consider untested approaches. "We know the safe path, but what if it's not enough? What would we try if we knew we couldn't fail?" This opens space for breakthrough thinking.

Backward Talk: "What's the worst that could happen if we try this?"
Forward Talk: "What's the best that could happen if we try this?"

When teams get stuck in risk-aversion, flip their focus to upside potential. "We've covered the downsides. What if everything goes right? What would that unlock for us?" This doesn't ignore the risks but balances fear with possibility, making bold moves feel worth considering.

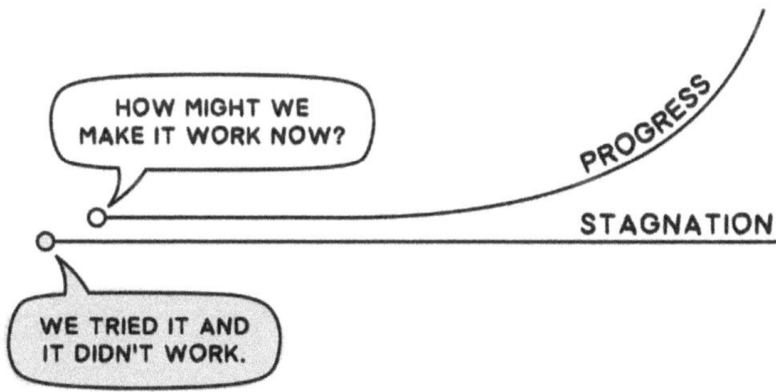

Milestone 5: Commit to Action

The final step is often where good conversations die—teams generate ideas but never follow through. These reframes ensure discussions translate into actions.

Backward Talk: "We should probably run this by [absent authority] before proceeding."
Forward Talk: "What decision can we make with the authority we have right now?"

When teams defer to absent decision-makers, identify the choices within the current scope. "We can't approve the budget, but could we agree on what we'd recommend?" This prevents decision paralysis while respecting hierarchal boundaries.

Backward Talk: "I still have concerns about this approach."
Forward Talk: "Are you willing to commit to this even though it wasn't your first choice?"

When someone disagrees with the final decision, focus on commitment despite disagreement. This is Amazon's "disagree and commit" principle—you can voice concerns during the discussion, but it's important to fully support the decision once it's made. "I know you preferred option B, but will you champion option A publicly and help make it successful?"

Backward Talk: "I think we're all aligned here."
Forward Talk: "What are we not aligned on that could derail this later?"

When alignment feels too easy, probe for hidden disagreements. "Before we commit, what concerns haven't been voiced? Where might we discover we're not actually aligned?" This surfaces issues before they become implementation problems.

Backward Talk: "That's not what we agreed on in the last meeting."
Forward Talk: "What did each of us understand we were agreeing to?"

When old decisions get relitigated, check whether there was actually a clear agreement in the first place. "If we're interpreting this differently, maybe our original agreement wasn't as clear as we thought. Let's figure out what we each heard." This reveals if teams need better decision-making processes, not just a better memory.

Backward Talk: "This sounds like a good plan—let's do it."
Forward Talk: "What exactly are we each committing to do, and by when?"

When teams settle for vague agreement, demand specific commitments. "A good plan isn't enough. Who owns what by which date? How will we know it's done?" This turns ideas into accountable actions.

Summary: Reframes per Milestone

Milestone 1: Initiate the Talk	
Backward Talk	**Forward Talk Reframe**
We don't want to open that can of worms.	What's the cost of leaving this unresolved for another month?
What's the point of speaking up? Nothing's going to change anyway.	What would prove that speaking up actually leads to action here?
Let's table this until our next meeting.	What's the smallest piece of this that we could resolve right now?
If we ignore this, it'll probably go away on its own.	What happens if we wait another month to address this?
The real conversation always happens after the meeting.	What prevents us from having this conversation right now?

Milestone 2: Keep an Open Mind	
Backward Talk	**Forward Talk Reframe**
Everyone seems comfortable with this approach.	Are we all comfortable or are we just not disagreeing out loud?
I don't want to be the one to bring this up.	Who else is thinking what I'm thinking but not saying it?
Don't be so negative about this.	What valid concerns are being raised here?
We all see this the same way.	What if we're completely wrong about what the real problem is?
We don't want this to turn into a debate.	What would someone who disagrees with us say about this situation?

Milestone 3: Explore the Root Cause	
Backward Talk	**Forward Talk Reframe**
We tried that approach before and it didn't work.	What's different now that might make this approach work?
We keep having the same problems over and over.	What pattern are we repeating, and how do we break it?
Whose fault is this?	Why does this same problem keep showing up in different forms?
Why didn't anyone speak up about this sooner?	What makes problems like this hard to spot until they've gotten big?
We just need to fix this specific issue.	If this problem were a symptom, what would the disease be?

Milestone 4: Generate Solutions	
Backward Talk	**Forward Talk Reframe**
That idea will never work here.	What would need to be true for this idea to succeed?
We already have too much on our plate.	What can we pause or stop to make room for what matters most?
No, that won't work because . . .	How might we build on it to make it work?
Let's stick to what we know works.	What's one bold move we haven't tried yet?
What's the worst that could happen if we try this?	What's the best that could happen if we try this?

Milestone 5: Commit to Action	
Backward Talk	**Forward Talk Reframe**
We should probably run this by [absent authority] before proceeding.	What decision can we make with the authority we have right now?
I still have concerns about this approach.	Are you willing to commit to this even though it wasn't your first choice?
I think we're all aligned here.	What are we not aligned on that could derail this later?
That's not what we agreed on in the last meeting.	What did each of us understand we were agreeing to?
This sounds like a good plan—let's do it.	What exactly are we committing to do, and by when?

Making It Work

Reframing conversations is a powerful technique to shift from Backward Talk to Forward Talk. Experiment with different reframes based on specific milestones, and use the table above as your guide.

Notice which reframes work best for your particular challenges. Some teams struggle with breaking the silence, while others have trouble addressing the root cause. Once you identify your team's specific sticking points, you can create your own reframes.

The key skill isn't crafting perfect questions but recognizing when conversations need redirecting—and having the courage to guide them forward. These reframes provide the language to transform stuck moments into breakthrough conversations, offering a practical way to put Forward Talk into action. But this is just the beginning.

CHAPTER 6

Map Your Conversational Patterns

Team conversations often feel like driving through an unfamiliar city and suddenly encountering a massive roundabout. If you miss the traffic signs, you can take the wrong exit or, worse, get stuck circling endlessly, passing the same landmarks with growing frustration. You're moving but getting nowhere.

Many teams fall into this trap, revisiting the same topics, stuck in familiar patterns, and mistaking motion for progress.

I created the Breaking the Conversational Loop Canvas to help teams escape this cycle. Based on the Forward Talk matrix, this visual tool helps teams identify their conversation pattern—blame, avoidance, or groupthink—and find a productive exit.

Understanding the Conversational Roundabout

The roundabout metaphor represents the four conversation patterns shaped by two key dimensions:

- **Time Orientation:** Are your conversations primarily focused on the past (what went wrong, who's responsible) or the future (what's possible, what's next)?
- **Conversation Depth:** Are your discussions addressing surface-level symptoms or diving into deeper root causes?

Use the Breaking the Conversational Loop Canvas to diagnose where your team is stuck and how to move forward.

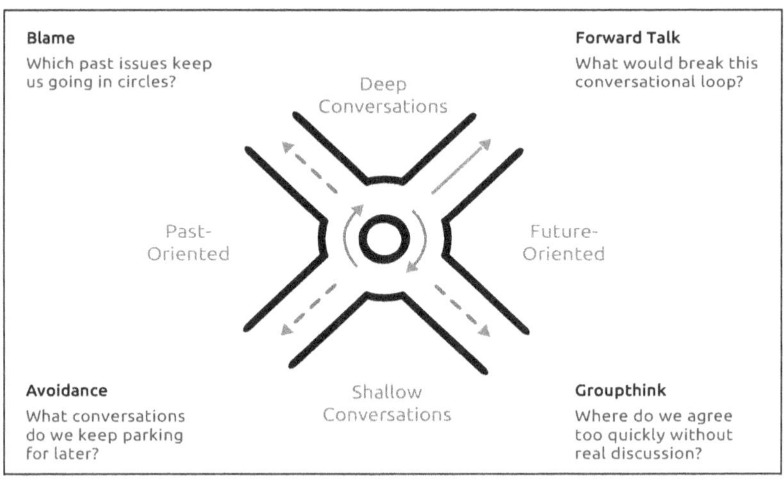

The Four Conversation Zones

The Blame Loop (Past-Oriented, Deep Conversations)

In the blame loop, teams dig deep into issues but fixate on past events and finding fault. "Why didn't you flag this sooner?" "We're repeating the same mistakes we made with the Johnson project." They circle endlessly through forensic analysis, getting nowhere.

The Avoidance Loop (Past-Oriented, Shallow Conversations)

When teams are stuck in avoidance, they acknowledge problems but don't want to talk about them. "Let's put that on the back burner for now." "We're not ready to have that conversation." They see the roundabout exists but refuse to navigate it.

The Groupthink Loop (Future-Oriented, Shallow Conversations)

When groupthink is the problematic loop, teams focus on the future but avoid tensions, creating false agreement. "I think we're all aligned here." "Great, sounds like we have a plan." They take what looks like an exit but continue circling instead, ending up right back where they started.

The Forward Talk Exit (Future-Oriented, Deep Conversations)

With Forward Talk, teams can take the exit, engaging deeply with real issues while maintaining future orientation. "What would need to be true for this to work?" "What do we need to solve so we can move forward?" This is the only lane that creates genuine progress.

How Teams Get Trapped

Most teams don't choose their lane consciously. They get pulled into patterns by the gravity of past habits:

- **Deadline pressure** leads to avoidance: "We don't have time to unpack this now."
- **Stress and conflict** trigger blame: "Someone needs to be held accountable for this mess."

- **Harmony addiction** creates groupthink: "Let's just agree and move on."

Teams burn energy circling the same conversations month after month without reaching their destination.

Using the Canvas for Team Diagnosis

The Breaking the Conversational Loop Canvas helps you spot recurring patterns so you can start shifting them. It gives teams a shared language to notice when they're stuck and the awareness to take the right exit, even when it's not the easiest. Here's how to navigate it:

Step 1: Set the Stage

Print a large version of the canvas or use a digital whiteboard. The goal isn't to solve everything, but to map where you're stuck.

Step 2: Map Your Routes

Have team members reflect, and note recent examples for each conversational loop:

- **Blame:** "What past issues keep us going in circles?" (e.g., the post-mortem that turned into a blame fest about missed deadlines)
- **Avoidance:** "What conversations do we keep parking for later?" (e.g., the client relationship everyone knows is deteriorating, but nobody discusses)
- **Groupthink:** "Where do we agree too quickly without real discussion?" (e.g., the strategy meeting where everyone nodded but left with different interpretations)

Once everyone has shared, place the examples in the relevant lanes of the canvas and group similar items together.

Step 3: Recognize the Cost of Circling

For each cluster, discuss as a team:

- How long have we been circling this topic?
- What's the actual cost—in time, trust, and energy—of staying in this lane?
- What keeps pulling us back into this roundabout?

Step 4: Identify Your Forward Talk Exits

Now focus on the exit lane: "What would break this conversational loop?" Work through the following as a team:

- List the conversations that need to be addressed or improved.
- Identify the patterns or habits that need to change.
- Frame the discussion around the future while still tackling the real issues, not just the surface-level symptoms.
- Review the reframes from Chapter 5. Which of these can help you exit unproductive conversations?

Step 5: Final Reflection

Wrap up by reflecting as a team:

- What have we learned about our conversation patterns?
- When and how will you try the Forward Talk approach?
- What's one pattern we need to monitor more closely in future conversations?
- How will we signal when we notice the team is circling instead of exiting?

Make It Stick

Treat the Breaking the Conversational Loop Canvas as a living tool. Keep it visible and use it in real time:

- **In meetings:** "I notice we're in the blame lane again. How do we get to Forward Talk?"
- **During planning:** "This feels like groupthink. What concerns aren't we surfacing?"
- **When tensions arise:** "We're avoiding the real issue. What conversation do we actually need to have?"

The goal isn't to avoid every roundabout—some topics require multiple discussions. The goal is intentional navigation. Once you know which lane you're in, you can choose where—and how—to exit.

Finding Your Way Forward

The Breaking the Conversational Loop Canvas doesn't solve your team's problems—it reveals patterns. Once you see the roundabout you're trapped in, you gain the power to choose a different route.

Every team has a choice: keep looping through the same conversations, or deliberately exit toward something better. Ready to stop circling and start progressing? You've got the map. Now it's time to lead your team out of the loop and into a conversation that actually goes somewhere.

But seeing the roundabout is just the beginning. Next, we'll explore in more depth the three types of conversational debt that trap teams and how to break free from them.

PART I RECAP

Stuck in Avoidance

In Summary:

Three behaviors kill conversations at work: avoidance (hoping problems will go away on their own), blame (pointing fingers instead of fixing things), and groupthink (pretending to look aligned when we're not). Conversational debt grows when we don't address what's really going on. Forward Talk helps you address the underlying issue and move the conversation forward.

Key Takeaways:

- People stay quiet because they don't think anything will change.
- Stop waiting for the perfect conditions to speak up. The longer you wait, the harder it gets.
- Someone needs to speak up first. That someone could be you.
- Diagnose where your team gets stuck. Some teams can't start hard conversations. Others get defensive too quickly.

PART II

Break Free from Debt

CHAPTER 7

The Cost of Silence

"Silence is a form of consent."

—David Thibodeau

The email that changed everything was only three lines long:

Team—after our recent meetings, I decided that all customer data will migrate to our ERP system. Timeline: 60 days.

This is nonnegotiable.

Questions offline only.

Astha stared at her screen in the break room of the newly acquired fintech startup where she was the lead data architect. She knew something her new corporate overlords didn't: Their "superior" system couldn't handle the complex financial instruments that her team had spent three years perfecting. The migration would corrupt transaction histories for at least forty thousand customers.

She'd tried to raise this issue several times during the integration planning meetings. Each time, she had been met with the same response: "We appreciate your concerns, but the decision has been made." In private conversations, her colleagues agreed with her assessment, but could see the problem she was facing. "Challenging him won't accomplish anything," one senior engineer confided over coffee. "He has the board's complete confidence. Nothing we say will change his mind."

So Astha made a quiet decision that would haunt her for months: to stop pushing back.

Sixty-seven days later, she sat silently in a tense all-hands meeting as that same CTO demanded answers while customer complaints flooded their support channels. "How did no one see this coming?" he shouted, pounding the table. "Someone should have flagged this risk!"

Astha had. Three times. In writing. But now, speaking up felt even more pointless; she knew nothing would change.

This is conversational debt in action—the accumulating cost of all the crucial conversations we don't have.

The Root of Conversational Debt

In Chapter 3, I introduced the concept of conversational debt and its crushing impact on teams and organizations. Now, we'll dig deeper into the three specific types of conversational debt and why they're so persistent.

Think about discovering a small humidity problem in your roof. At first, it seems innocuous—maybe you notice a tiny water stain on the ceiling during heavy rain. Easy to ignore, right? But humidity doesn't stay contained. It spreads through insulation, warps wood, and creates conditions for mold. Before you know it, you're not just patching a leak—you're replacing the entire roof and refinishing the entire room.

Just think back to Astha. The first time she raised concerns, she was shut down. The second time, she was ignored. By the third, she barely had the energy to try. Each moment of silence didn't just represent a missed opportunity—it increased the cost of speaking up next time. By the time the system failed and the fallout began, it was too late to go back.

To understand why small issues become so expensive, we need to look at how conversational debt compounds:

Conversational Debt =
Unresolved Issues × Productivity Loss × Time

This formula isn't meant for a precise calculation, but it will help your team connect the dots between silence and its impact.

The more unresolved issues you carry,

↓

the more they drag down your performance,

↓

the longer you wait to address them,

↓

and the more costly they become.

Think about a conversation you've avoided in the past month. What has it cost you—or your team—so far? Where might small tensions be compounding into larger risks?

While these tensions may seem small at the outset, in retrospect it's easy to see the compounding interest of the conversations we avoid or manage poorly.

The Three Types of Conversational Debt

My research with over 5,350 professionals revealed that conversational debt doesn't accumulate randomly. It builds in three distinct but interconnected ways:

- **Alignment Debt:** A striking 70.1 percent of respondents strongly agreed that people frequently say "yes" even if they aren't on board. Over half (57.4 percent) said their teams often skip hard conversations just to feel aligned.
- **Belonging Debt:** Many executives engage in a pervasive "playing the game" pattern—avoiding conflict or pretending to align while privately harboring different views. This surfaces in behaviors like qualified speech ("This might be stupid, but . . . ") and post-meeting corridor conversations. Teams may feel like they belong to the organization, but can't contribute effectively.
- **Collaboration Debt:** This type of debt is perhaps the most telling for organizations that are focused on results, where almost 70 percent of people reported that projects stall because most conversations focus on assigning blame and identifying who's at fault. This translates directly to missed deadlines, budget overruns, and diminished quality.

The Conversational Debt Spiral

What makes conversational debt so dangerous is that it doesn't just accumulate—it accelerates. The three types of debt feed off one another, creating a downward spiral that traps teams in the exact patterns they're trying to escape.

Think of it like a psychological tornado. Poor alignment creates confusion, which prompts people to avoid difficult clarifying conversations (belonging debt), which leads to endless circular discussions without clear decisions (collaboration debt), which creates even worse team conditions (alignment debt).

Round and round it goes, each rotation making the next one faster and more destructive.

This spiral explains why teams get magnetically pulled into Backward Talk:

1. **Blame:** When alignment debt mounts—when no one is sure who's truly committed—teams default to forensic analysis. Who screwed up? Which departments were supposed to do what? Energy flows toward the past instead of into the future.
2. **Avoidance:** As belonging debt increases, people learn that raising concerns feels risky and futile—it seems safer to stay quiet and hope someone else will speak up. Conversations stay safely in the shallows, while real issues fester beneath the surface.

3. **Groupthink:** When collaboration debt stalls decision-making, teams start rubber-stamping anything that looks like progress. Surface-level agreement becomes more valuable than genuine problem-solving.

These Backward Talk patterns continue to build all three types of debt, creating a self-reinforcing cycle that gradually erodes team effectiveness.

In Astha's organization, everyone made the same calculation: Speaking up felt futile rather than productive. However, silence has its own cost—one that accumulates quietly, until it becomes crushing. Even if the outcome of speaking up is unpredictable, I can assure you that doing nothing will keep things exactly as they are—or make them even worse.

But don't worry, I won't leave you spinning in this tornado. Later, in Chapter 12, you'll get the Conversational Debt Spiral Canvas—a diagnostic tool to map exactly where your team is caught and how to chart the escape route.

The Regret That Never Fades

You're probably wondering what conversational debt has to do with you personally. You might think that avoiding that performance discussion or staying quiet during strategic planning won't impact your life outside work. But silence—especially the kind we justify in the moment—has a way of lingering. Let me summarize it in one word: **regret**.

But often our regret isn't because we stayed silent—it's because we gave up.

Daniel Pink discovered this by analyzing more than 23,000 regrets from people across 109 countries. His research reveals something that should fundamentally change how you think about difficult conversations: **We regret the things we didn't do far more than the things we did.**[14]

While people in their twenties tend to regret actions and inactions equally, this balance shifts significantly with age. By their thirties and beyond, people are twice as likely to regret what they didn't do as what they did.

Pink's research identified four universal regrets: foundation regrets (failures of responsibility), boldness regrets (missed opportunities to take risks), moral regrets (ethical failures), and connection regrets (neglected relationships).[15] Two of these directly explain why conversational debt becomes personally expensive:

- *Boldness regrets* center on missed opportunities to speak up—not voicing concerns about flawed strategies, not challenging unrealistic timelines, or not offering valuable perspectives. People consistently regret not speaking up far more than they regret having spoken up, even if their input was unwelcome.
- *Moral regrets* involve failing to act on one's personal values—staying silent when someone was treated unfairly, not advocating for quality or safety standards, or watching problematic decisions unfold without intervening. These carry particular psychological weight because they involve questions of character and integrity.

What makes both types painful is their open-ended nature. Unlike action regrets—with concrete outcomes you can learn from—inaction regrets create infinite "what-if" scenarios that can linger with us for decades.

And this doesn't just happen at work. The cost of unspoken words shows up in our personal lives, too. One person I interviewed shared: *"I mishandled telling a friend they couldn't come to my wedding as I didn't have enough space. Didn't think they would mind so much. They did mind. They were offended. Not spoken to me since. It's been sixteen years."*

That's the cruel irony in how we calculate conversational risk: The choice that feels emotionally safe—staying silent to avoid conflict—consistently creates a deeper, lasting psychological cost. In contrast, speaking up despite uncertainty typically generates manageable, time-limited consequences that can become learning experiences rather than sources of ongoing regret.

The conversation you're debating whether or not to have isn't just about increasing team effectiveness. According to Pink's research, it's about the person you'll be proud to have been when you look back years from now. We unconsciously choose to carry decades of personal regret rather than experience minutes of social discomfort.

Yet the price of silence isn't always paid immediately. Sometimes, it's a cost we carry quietly for years—only realizing too late how much it has shaped the life we've lived, or damaged the relationships we've lost.

Now that you understand the organizational and personal costs of conversational debt, it's time to assess your own. The Conversational Debt Assessment that follows can help uncover hidden patterns across the three types of debt.

Your Conversational Debt Assessment

Your team needs to identify its conversational debt before addressing it. Unlike financial debt, there's no statement showing what you owe—but the costs are real, and often higher than expected.

I've developed a research-based assessment that helps teams identify their specific debt patterns across the three types of conversational debt. This reflective tool gives you immediate insights into where your team is accumulating this debt and which areas need attention first.

Use this assessment to identify patterns of conversational debt across the three types: avoidance, groupthink, and blame. For each set of statements, rate how often these patterns show up in your team, from 1 (rarely true) to 5 (often true). Then total your score for each category.

Alignment Debt

We regularly make decisions even though not all voices have been heard.	
People avoid challenging the group's direction even when they have private doubts.	
We prioritize quick alignment over exploring multiple options thoroughly.	
We often hear "That's not what we agreed on," even after supposed alignment meetings.	
We choose ideas based on likeability rather than their merit or potential impact.	
Subtotal	

Belonging Debt

We postpone addressing tensions until they become urgent or unmanageable.	
Difficult topics are routinely "parked" or "taken offline" instead of being resolved in the moment.	
Team members hesitate to bring up risks or unpopular perspectives.	
We readily offer appreciative feedback but struggle with constructive criticism.	
We default to consensus building, even when it dilutes stronger individual ideas.	
"This is how we do things here" is often used to shut down uncomfortable discussions.	
Subtotal	

Collaboration Debt

When things go wrong, our first instinct is to identify who dropped the ball.	
We tend to get stuck rehashing past decisions rather than focusing on what to do next.	
Team members are quick to justify their positions rather than explore collaborative solutions.	
Simple decisions require multiple meetings because we keep debating who makes the final call.	
People blame unclear goals or decisions on others instead of seeking clarity together.	
Subtotal	

Score Range (per category)

5–10 = Low Conversational Debt

11–17 = Moderate Conversational Debt

18–25 = High Conversational Debt

Your total score shows how conversational debt is affecting your team right now. The real risk isn't your current score, but what happens if these patterns continue unchecked.

Low Conversational Debt (5–10 per category): Your team likely has strong communication foundations. Still, low scores don't mean no risk—conversational debt can accumulate quickly if issues go unchecked. Use this as an opportunity to reinforce healthy habits and stay alert for early warning signs.

Moderate Conversational Debt (11–17 per category): Your team is showing clear signs of communication strain. You're not in crisis yet, but patterns are forming that will become expensive if left unaddressed. This is the optimal time to intervene—problems are visible but still manageable. Focus on addressing the highest-scoring category first.

High Conversational Debt (18–25 per category): Your team is carrying a heavy conversational burden that's likely affecting performance, morale, and decision-making. A high score means avoidance, blame, and groupthink patterns have become entrenched. Turning this around will require a structural intervention, not quick fixes.

Your scores reveal where your team's conversational patterns may be creating problems. High avoidance scores often lead to crises that result from ignored warnings. High groupthink scores usually mean diverse perspectives are being silenced. And high blame scores indicate energy wasted on rehashing past failures rather than finding better solutions.

Your Path Forward

Now that you understand your debt profile, you have two options:

Option 1: Jump to Immediate Solutions. If you want practical tools you can implement right away—or you don't have time to dig into the root causes—skip ahead to Part IV: Forward Talk in Action. You'll find multiple techniques to shift conversations from Backward Talk patterns to Forward Talk progress.

Option 2: Tackle the Root Causes. If you want to understand why these patterns keep recurring and how to address them systematically, dive into the next three chapters:

- Chapter 8 reveals how alignment debt creates the illusion of agreement while teams pull in different directions.
- Chapter 9 exposes how belonging debt turns harmony into a weapon against authentic dialogue.
- Chapter 10 shows how collaboration debt makes teamwork feel like theater instead of progress.

The conversations you're avoiding right now are already costing you more than you think. Understanding the root causes will help you prevent debt from reaccumulating in the future.

CHAPTER 8

The Illusion of Alignment

"The single biggest problem in communication is the illusion that it has taken place."

—George Bernard Shaw

Steve, the CEO of Algonich, a fast-growth financial startup, believed his leadership team was perfectly aligned. After months of strategic planning, they had all committed to the same vision: becoming truly customer-centric.

And Steve wasn't wrong—I heard that exact phrase in every department when I was hired to facilitate a post-mortem. But alignment had turned out to be an illusion, and that illusion was on full display when I conducted stakeholder interviews.

Operations thought "customer-centric" meant speed—streamlining processes and cutting wait times.

Compliance was certain it meant protection, such as adding security measures and verification steps.

Marketing believed it meant personalization through better customer data.

Operations was eliminating steps to move faster, while Compliance was adding layers that slowed everything down. They were aligned in principle and at war in practice.

This chapter looks at why teams often think they're aligned when in reality they're not. We'll unpack how vague language, shallow agreement, and top-down direction create the illusion of alignment—and how that leads to confusion, delay, and frustration down the line.

You'll learn how to spot signs of alignment debt, why forced agreement rarely works, and what healthy alignment looks like: clear priorities, shared purpose, and real commitment—even when people disagree.

The Alignment Trap

Algonich's story isn't unique—it's the norm. Most leaders believe they've achieved alignment when they've only created the illusion of it.

High-growth strategy expert Dr. Rebecca Homkes, from London Business School, uncovered this pervasive pattern after studying more than four hundred companies.[16] In one case, a professional services CEO was convinced her communication strategy was working perfectly. She repeated the firm's strategy and priorities to her management team every month. When their employee engagement survey showed 84 percent of staff were "clear on organizational priorities," she felt vindicated.

But when Homkes asked the leadership team a simple follow-up question—"What are your company's top three to five priorities?"—the illusion of alignment quickly unraveled. The answers varied widely. There was little overlap, and fewer than a third of the executives could name even two of the company's five strategic priorities.

This wasn't an outlier—it's the typical example of the alignment trap. In Homkes's broader research involving over eleven thousand senior managers, only one-third could accurately name their company's top three priorities, and just half could agree on the number one.[17] Even more striking, only 50 percent of the executives responsible for setting company objectives could identify them clearly.

How can you expect people to align if even those who set the goals can't remember what they are?

Here's what most leaders get wrong about alignment: They think it means convincing people to embrace their vision, getting all the ducks in a row behind their strategy. But this perspective turns alignment into a persuasion exercise rather than a commitment-building process.

Corporate America has created an entire alignment industry around this flawed premise. Companies spend millions on town halls, cascading goals, vision statements, and alignment retreats—elaborate exercises designed to get everyone "on the same page" with leadership's predetermined direction.

The problem isn't how often leaders communicate—90 percent of middle managers say leaders communicate strategy frequently enough. But as Homkes puts it: "Communication does not equal understanding; shared context does. Volume of communication doesn't create comprehension."

Think about BlackBerry, the device that was so addictive that Obama fought to keep his when he became president.[18] When the iPhone launched, BlackBerry's executives dismissed the threat and convinced everyone, "We'll be fine," forcing everyone to align with their perspective. But their engineers saw the future coming—touchscreen devices, apps, and a completely different approach to mobile computing.

BlackBerry went from 50 percent to 1 percent market share[19] because forced alignment prevented the company from adapting to reality. By demanding agreement rather than encouraging challenge, leadership shut down the very input that could have helped them adapt. It's a clear warning: Forcing shallow alignment instead of wrestling with hard truths is corporate suicide.

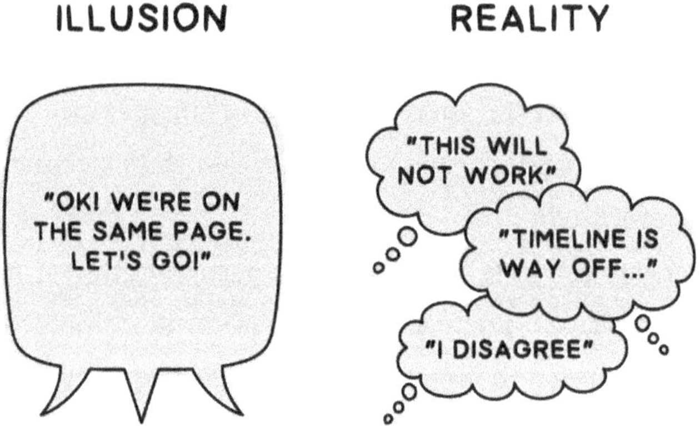

The Alignment Gurus' Seductive Promise

The corporate alignment industry sells a seductive promise: With the right processes, frameworks, and communication strategies, you can get everyone rowing in the same direction. The assumption is that misalignment stems from poor communication or insufficient buy-in to leadership's vision, and this creates a multibillion-dollar industry of:

- **Cascading goal frameworks** that ensure everyone's objectives ladder-up to leadership priorities

- **Vision communication campaigns** designed to build excitement around leadership's strategic direction
- **Alignment surveys** that measure how well people understand and support the company's direction

All of this misses the fundamental point: True alignment doesn't come from convincing people to support your plan. It comes from building shared commitment to a direction that everyone helps shape and wants to pursue.

Companies that operate with a sense of purpose beyond just meeting their quarterly goals outperform the S&P 500 by a factor of 14.[20] Yet most alignment efforts get this backward—they cascade goals instead of building a shared understanding of why those goals matter. When people understand the "why," they can make aligned decisions even when leaders are not in the room.

How the Alignment Trap Drives Backward Talk

Top-down alignment doesn't just limit creativity—it reshapes how teams talk. When the goal is to fall in line with a predetermined direction, two destructive patterns emerge:

- **Primary pattern: avoidance.** When alignment becomes about supporting predetermined conclusions, people learn to avoid voicing any concerns that might challenge the direction:
  - "Let's assume we're all on the same page here."
  - "I'm sure leadership has thought this through."
  - "We can work out the details later."

- **Secondary pattern: groupthink.** When dissent feels like disloyalty to leadership's vision, teams rush to superficial consensus:

- "We need to present a united front on this."
- "Let's all just agree this is the direction."
- "It seems we're all finally aligned here."

The illusion of alignment may seem harmless, but it leads to costly breakdowns in trust, execution, and follow-through.

How Alignment Debt Manifests

We often think misalignment is easy to observe, but it rarely is. Alignment debt doesn't typically appear as arguments or dramatic blowups. Instead, it shows up in subtle ways—teams seem to agree in meetings but work toward different goals afterward. Here are the most common signs of alignment debt:

- **Shallow agreements:** Teams hurry to reach a consensus without addressing real concerns. My research shows 56 percent of respondents think "rushing to quick agreements" is why conversations fail. People publicly support decisions that they question in private.
- **Fake support:** Team members say "yes" but don't actually commit to action. Nearly 70 percent of professionals in my study said "nodding but not following through" is the main indicator of false alignment.
- **Being a "team player":** People avoid raising concerns just to be seen as cooperative. As one engineering director told me, "In our culture, raising concerns makes you look negative. It's safer to agree now and explain delays later."
- **Convergent research:** Team members ask AI the same questions. They all get similar answers and think they've

done diverse research. Nobody questions the direction because everyone's information matches—but that's only because they consulted the same oracle.

- **Vague language:** Teams use unclear terms that everyone interprets differently. Words like "agile," "customer-centric," or "data-driven" mean various things to various people. This creates the illusion of alignment when people are actually agreeing to completely different things.

Here's how alignment debt compares to healthy alignment:

Alignment Debt	Healthy Alignment
Everyone nods but leaves with different interpretations	Leaders actively confirm understanding—alignment is challenged, not assumed
People align with leaders, not with the purpose	Teams align around a shared purpose, not personalities
Post-meeting talks reveal what people really think	Real conversations happen in the actual meeting
Decisions get quietly revisited weeks later	Commitment beyond agreement: "It wasn't my choice, but I'll support it"
Vague language (like "customer-centric") allows for multiple interpretations	Specific examples are used to show what a direction really means
Conflicting priorities are left unattended	Clear trade-offs: "Quality even over speed"

Real alignment doesn't mean everyone agrees on everything. It means people commit to the same goal even when they have different views.

Goodbye Alignment Debt: IBM's Comeback

When Lou Gerstner became IBM's leader in 1993, he expected to find a strategy problem. Instead, he discovered something worse: executives who thought they were on the same page, but weren't.

Every leader could recite IBM's mission. Everyone said customer success was important. But when Gerstner started asking questions about specifics, the gap in understanding became evident.

Engineering was building for one thing. Sales was pitching something else. Marketing had its own plan. The word "success" meant something different to everyone.

As Gerstner famously said, "The last thing IBM needs right now is a vision."[21] What executives needed most was to listen to customers and break down internal silos.

The CEO realized that culture is everything. While many experts suggested breaking IBM up into independent "Baby Blues," Gerstner had a different instinct. He wanted decentralized, faster decision-making, but also to recover IBM's main strength: offering complete solutions. He knew customers found IBM difficult to work with.

Gerstner redefined IBM's priorities, starting with the customer. He created a simple framework with three pillars: recommit to quality, become easier to work with, and regain market leadership. Every department had to align on this, using the same metrics and language.

Change didn't happen overnight, but it was systematic. Within six months, misalignment became visible instead of hidden. Teams could see where their efforts conflicted with others. Within a year, IBM started working as one company, putting customers first.

Gerstner learned that real alignment isn't about inspiring words, but about agreeing on how you measure success.

Spotting Your Alignment Debt

Use these questions to start honest team discussions. Look for places where team members don't answer with a clear "yes" or where opinions differ—these reveal alignment debt.

Focus on one area at a time where your team hesitates or disagrees. Begin with the most obvious gaps or where conversations feel most urgent.

Purpose Alignment

- Does everyone on your team know and understand your company's purpose?
- Can team members connect their daily work to your organizational purpose?
- Does your purpose guide decision-making during conflicts or trade-offs?

Values Alignment

- Do team members use the organization's core values to make decisions?
- When values conflict with expedience, do people consistently choose values?
- Can people explain how the values apply to specific work situations?

Priority Alignment

- Can everyone name the top three organizational priorities without hesitation?
- Do people make decisions that align with these priorities?
- When priorities conflict, does everyone know which ones take precedence?

Behavioral Alignment

- Is there consistency between what behaviors your organization rewards and what it claims to value?
- Do people know exactly what behaviors will help them succeed?
- Do leaders model the same behaviors that they expect from others?

Most alignment problems aren't caused by a lack of communication but by the illusion of agreement.[22] People use identical words but walk away with entirely different interpretations and intentions.

In the next chapter, we'll explore how belonging debt leads teams to prioritize being liked over being honest, and what this is costing them.

The Tyranny of Harmony

"The most exhausting thing in life is being insincere."

—Anne Morrow Lindbergh

The architectural studio's culture was legendary. The four partners called themselves "the family," and even though two of them had retired, they still attended every final design review. Team members celebrated each project and ensured no one ever left a meeting feeling criticized.

Harmony ruled every interaction. It was the kind of environment that won "Best Place to Work" awards.

However, issues emerged when a $12 million project fell dramatically behind schedule. During the brutal post-mortem, the truth emerged: Three team members had spotted the problems months earlier, but had stayed silent.

The structural engineer had privately worried about viability.

The project manager knew the timeline was unrealistic.

The junior architect felt the design wouldn't meet code requirements.

But none of them spoke up. As Paul, the engineer, told me during the retrospective, "One of the founders was so proud of the design—and let's just say he didn't exactly have a track record of loving feedback."

The company's greatest strength—making everyone feel good—had become their greatest weakness. Their strong family vibe silenced dissent in the name of keeping everyone happy.

When teams chase harmony at the expense of honesty, they accumulate belonging debt—a culture where speaking up feels disloyal and niceness overrides truth. We've turned psychological safety into a catch-all solution that often backfires, creating fragile environments where people nod along, avoid conflict, and suppress concerns to maintain a false sense of belonging.

The result is poor decisions, stalled innovation, and unresolved tensions that eventually explode. The path forward isn't more comfort—it's more courage. Your team must be willing to take risks, offer dissent, and choose honesty over harmony.

The Safety Bubble That Backfires

Psychological safety is the belief that you can speak up, make mistakes, or share a dissenting view without fear of embarrassment, rejection, or punishment.

Here's where I need to be brutally honest: I've been challenging the psychological safety orthodoxy for years, but the groupthink around it has only gotten worse.

For ten years, psychological safety has been central to my work. My Culture Design Canvas includes it as one of ten building blocks.[23]

I've run hundreds of workshops teaching leaders and teams how to build psychologically safe environments.

But here's what happens: Organizations often call me in after they've spent big money on psychological safety training, only to see no change, or worse, to watch it backfire.

Psychological safety has become corporations' ultimate magic cure-all. Teams underperforming? Build psychological safety. People not speaking up? More psychological safety. Ask ChatGPT for help with any team problem? You guessed it—psychological safety.

It's the ultimate irony: We've created groupthink around a concept designed to prevent groupthink. Psychological safety has become an overused concept that's lost its meaning.

Why did this happen? Because it sells. There's a multimillion-dollar industry of workshops, books, and training programs built on a simple idea: Make people feel safe, and they'll speak up.

It's like the old saying about IBM[24]—no one gets fired for recommending psychological safety.

But people don't always behave as we expect, so we should adapt frameworks to fit reality, not force reality to fit our frameworks. When people keep saying "it's not safe" and avoid speaking up,[25] maybe our approach is the problem. Instead of blaming others for the environment we've created, let's change our approach.

When Safety Becomes a Weapon

Intentionally or not, psychological safety is often weaponized against the very outcomes it was meant to create. Much like Frankenstein's monster, this concept has evolved far beyond its original intent, and people use it as a shield against participation:

- "This place isn't safe for me to share my real concerns."

- "I can't speak up because we don't have enough psychological safety."
- "The leadership needs to create a safer environment before I'll contribute."

Leaders also weaponize it through magical thinking, declaring, "This is a safe space," as if saying so creates instant trust.

But here's the biggest weaponization: We've stripped away individual agency. We've turned psychological safety into something people expect others to provide, rather than recognizing it as the communal result of everyone's courageous behaviors.

It's the ultimate chicken-and-egg problem. People say they won't speak up because it's unsafe, but it will never become safe if no one takes a risk and speaks up. We've created a waiting game where teams expect the perfect conditions, which can only be achieved by the very behaviors they're avoiding.

That's why Forward Talk focuses on breaking the three patterns that keep teams stuck—blame, avoidance, and groupthink—by building individual and collective agency to act even when conditions aren't ideal. Waiting for the "right moment" only increases conversational debt.

When Talking Feels Pointless

The environment matters, but not as much as we think it does. Team members themselves are also important to the equation.

My research identified three distinct groups of individuals when it comes to speaking up:

1. **Personality-driven contributors:** people who speak up regardless of environmental safety

2. **Natural avoiders:** those who rarely share their thoughts, even in spaces that are clearly safe
3. **Environment-sensitive participants:** people whose willingness to speak up depends on the safety signals they perceive

Psychological safety primarily affects the third group—those whose participation depends on safety cues. That's only about one-third of your team, yet we've treated it as a universal solution, then wondered why the other two-thirds of people still don't fully engage.

Remember the Pointlessness Paradox from Chapter 1? People don't just avoid difficult conversations because they're afraid—they avoid them because they believe speaking up is pointless:

- "It won't change anything." (64.6 percent)
- "I don't want to damage the relationship." (49.7 percent)
- "I'm not sure the other person is open to feedback." (48.6 percent)

Notice the pattern? It's not fear of consequences—it's futility about the *relationship itself.* People think:

- "This person won't be open to hearing this."
- "They'll just get defensive."
- "The team will think I'm being negative."
- "Leadership has already made up their minds."

Curious to understand what drives the personality-driven contributors, I asked Hogan Assessments to identify the traits of people who consistently speak up. Their analysis revealed that these individuals score high on ambition, boldness, inquisitiveness, and imagination, while scoring lower on cautiousness and dutifulness.

They're willing to take social risks regardless of environmental conditions.

As Ryne Sherman, Chief Science Officer at Hogan, told me, "Leaders often overestimate the effects of organizational policy and procedure on employee behavior. While creating a psychologically safe environment does have an impact on employee willingness to speak up and challenge authority, personality also plays an important role. Some people are willing to question orders, challenge authority, and prioritize their own beliefs over external directives."[26]

Howard and Cogswell's "Left Side of Courage" study delivers a final blow to environmental determinism.[27] They surveyed nearly eight hundred workers and found that traits like grit and a proactive personality are far better predictors of workplace courage than environmental factors like an empowering leadership team or supportive cultures.

Even more strikingly, people's beliefs about the risks of speaking up weren't significant predictors of whether they actually did it.

The implications are staggering: We've been trying to adjust our environments when the real drivers of change are individual agency and choice.

The uncomfortable truth is that excessively nice cultures create their own toxicity. When we prioritize comfort over growth, harmony over truth, and protection over challenge—what Jonathan Haidt and Greg Lukianoff call "safetyism"[28]—authentic dialogue becomes impossible.

That's what I call the Psychological Safety Bubble. Some organizations and consultants are putting too much emphasis on safety—not on taking risks—and it's backfiring. I'm here to pop the bubble.

UNADDRESSED ISSUES...

...WILL SURFACE EVENTUALLY

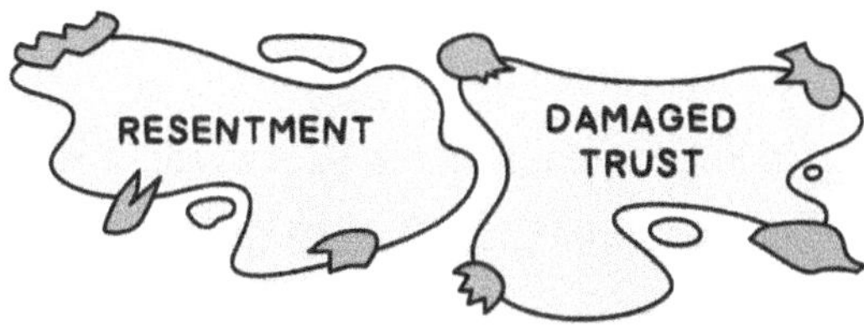

How Belonging Debt Drives Backward Talk

When teams prioritize artificial harmony over authentic dialogue, belonging debt accumulates through predictable patterns:

- **Primary pattern: groupthink.** Teams prioritize consensus above truth, developing superficial agreement patterns that suppress authentic dialogue:
  - "Let's not rock the boat."
  - "We all need to be on the same page."
  - "This is how we do things here."

This future-focused but surface-level pattern creates an illusion of progress while preventing the robust conversations needed for genuine innovation.

- **Secondary pattern: avoidance.** The fear of disrupting group harmony leads teams to sidestep difficult topics entirely:
  - "Let's table this discussion for now."
  - "Maybe we should discuss this offline."
  - "We don't need to get into that right now."

These avoidance patterns prevent teams from addressing issues when they're small and manageable, allowing them to grow into significant problems.

This is how belonging debt drives Backward Talk: When teams avoid short-term discomfort, they trade truth for harmony—and move further away from trust, clarity, and progress.

How Belonging Debt Manifests

Belonging debt reveals itself through subtle patterns that teams often mistake for healthy culture:

- **Quick and shallow agreements:** Teams rush to consensus without thoroughly exploring other options or implications—the desire to appear cooperative overrides rigorous evaluation. Everyone says, "Great idea!" but nobody asks the hard questions.
- **Giving only appreciative feedback:** People readily give praise but withhold concerns. This creates false confidence while preventing necessary growth.
- **Disagreement equals disloyalty:** Organizations develop cultures where challenging ideas feels like attacking the culture. Disagreement becomes betrayal.

- **Trust displacement:** People turn to AI to verify their teammates' recommendations instead of addressing concerns with them directly. Teams seem to get along well on the surface, but individuals quietly fact-check one another because they trust AI more than their teammates.[29]
- **Conforming pressure:** Team members develop unspoken tests—either you fit in or don't belong. This tribal dynamic forces people to suppress unique viewpoints in favor of social acceptance.

The most revealing sign is when questions about risks or potential problems are met with nervous laughter or a quick dismissal—that's belonging debt in action.

Here's how belonging debt compares to healthy belonging:

Belonging Debt	Healthy Belonging
"We're like family," but people walk on eggshells	People care more about the work than fitting in
Everyone agrees too quickly	Open disagreement about ideas while respecting people
Challenging ideas feels like attacking the culture	Challenging ideas is not just welcomed but expected
Those who raise concerns are labeled as "negative"	"Devil's advocate" role is intentionally integrated into discussions
Only appreciative feedback gets shared	Both constructive and appreciative feedback flow regularly
Conflict is avoided to preserve harmony	Problems are addressed early on
Promotion of a safe environment	Promotion of courageous behaviors—individual and collective

Belonging debt comes from more than just team dynamics—it also results from mixed messages from leadership. When leaders reward harmony over honesty, quickly dismiss concerns, or get defensive, they show that speaking up isn't really safe—even if they talk about psychological safety.

Creating healthy belonging means showing that disagreement is normal and welcome. It means asking to hear the tough questions and responding with curiosity instead of control. As one senior leader told me, "If everyone agrees with me too quickly, I worry I've made it unsafe to disagree." This approach creates genuine belonging.

Canceling Belonging Debt: Best Buy's Turnaround

When Hubert Joly became Best Buy's CEO in 2012, the company was in trouble with declining sales, increased online competition, and low morale. The retailer needed a significant turnaround to survive, and the consensus was overwhelming. Everyone—board members, consultants, industry experts, and business media—gave the same advice: "Cut costs, close stores, fire people." This was the standard playbook for struggling retailers.

Anyone suggesting a different approach seemed out of touch. But Joly challenged groupthink and *took a bold move*: He decided to honor Best Buy's legacy of great customer service and store expertise.

Joly spent his first week working in a store wearing the typical blue shirt uniform and a "CEO in Training" badge. This wasn't just for show. He was committed to listening to employees. He said, "The front line is where you learn about a company's culture. The front line is the one who will tell you everything you need to know. After all, they are the face of your company. Take care of your employees, and they'll take care of your business."

What he found changed everything. The employees that the experts wanted to fire were actually assets. They understood what the consultants had missed: that many customers wanted a place to touch, feel the products, and ask questions.

To turn things around, Joly encouraged store managers to reflect on their strengths, trust their instincts, and create "magic."[30]

Store managers took a risk by sharing their honest thoughts during this difficult time—their insights had been ignored for years by previous leaders. But the risk of speaking up was nothing compared to the risk of losing not just their jobs, but the whole organization.

Employees began focusing beyond just understanding their customers' needs. They helped clients achieve their dreams. Their goal became enriching people's lives through technology. This created a strong sense of belonging where the employees—not the leaders—became the heroes.

The result? Best Buy didn't just survive—it thrived. The company that everyone thought would fail became a model for successful retail transformation. Not because they followed groupthink, but because they dared to challenge it.

Recognizing Your Belonging Debt

Belonging debt silently undermines team trust and performance. Use the questions below to find gaps between your perceived and actual culture. Reflect alone or as a team to identify where hidden tensions or conflict avoidance might be limiting your potential.

Social Courage

- Do people challenge decisions and leaders without fear of retaliation?
- Are mistakes treated as learning opportunities rather than failures?
- Do team members take interpersonal risks when it matters?

Feedback Culture

- Do people regularly give each other honest feedback, not just praise?
- Is constructive criticism seen as helpful rather than hurtful?
- Do team members actively seek feedback instead of avoiding it?

Rituals and Connection

- Do people participate in team rituals because they want to, or because they feel they have to?
- When someone opts out of a team event, are they treated differently afterward?
- Do people share real challenges during team check-ins, or just safe, positive updates?

Authentic Participation

- Do people bring their real concerns to team discussions?
- Are diverse perspectives genuinely explored, not just acknowledged?
- Can team members be themselves without conforming to group expectations?

When your team hesitates to speak up, it often signals that people don't feel seen or heard. These moments are perfect opportunities for meaningful conversations about belonging.

Don't just focus on psychological safety—making it safe to speak. Also promote psychological courage—the willingness to raise difficult topics and challenge groupthink.

Excessive harmony can paralyze your team. When avoiding conflict matters more than honesty, problems grow until they explode. True belonging means having the courage to disagree respectfully.

Next, we'll explore how this problem leads to collaboration debt, where teamwork becomes more about appearances than actual progress.

CHAPTER 10

The Collaboration Theater

"A camel is a horse designed by committee."

—Alec Issigonis

Silvina was excited about her new project. As head of the culture committee, she saw planning the company retreat as her chance to celebrate employees.

Her team spent weeks crafting a thoughtful agenda with meaningful team activities, an inspiring speaker, and sessions based on employee input. They surveyed everyone and designed a retreat that people would value.

Then came an unexpected email from the CEO: "We need to discuss the retreat planning. The leadership team feels left out."

This confused Silvina. The culture committee had been *explicitly* tasked to represent employee voices, not executives' preferences. Now, leadership wanted to weigh in on everything.

What followed was a collaboration nightmare.

While claiming to only "provide guidance," the leadership team scheduled meeting after meeting. They criticized the venue as "too casual," insisted activities be "more strategic," and questioned the speaker's credentials.

Each critique came with a disclaimer: "Of course, this is still the culture committee's decision."

But no one knew what that meant. When Silvina raised concerns, the CFO responded, "Are we not allowed opinions?" When executives directly modified vendor contracts, the committee wondered if they had any control left.

After three months and fourteen meetings, the retreat left everyone unhappy. The committee felt ignored while leadership blamed "lack of ownership" for poor execution.

The feedback surveys were terrible.

Later, the CEO summoned Silvina to his office. "The feedback is awful," he said. "How did your committee let this happen? This was supposed to be your project."

Silvina was left picking up the pieces of the mess she never made.

The initiative had fallen victim to the collaboration trap. When it failed, nobody looked at what went wrong—they just looked for someone to blame.

This scenario is collaboration debt in action: When teams lose their ability to work together effectively, they fall into the blame reflex, pointing fingers at other departments, partners, or colleagues.

It's what builds up when there's constant coordination but little progress—when decisions stall, trust erodes, and no one is quite sure who owns what.

In this chapter, you'll learn why collaboration often fails and what healthy collaboration looks like. We'll explore the psychological traps that sabotage teamwork, the signals that your team may be in collaboration debt, and the real cost of not addressing those tensions.

The Cult of Collaboration

We've created a cult of collaboration that's costing us dearly—and it's built on a fundamental misunderstanding of how teamwork works.

Research shows that 81 percent of people believe collaboration is critical, and 71 percent think their managers are making it a priority.[31] Yet, study after study reveals that most collaborative efforts fail spectacularly. The reason? Leaders fail to design the conditions to make it possible.

For decades, business experts have glorified collaboration as the key to productivity and innovation. However, here's the uncomfortable truth: There was never much evidence that collaboration was the solution, and now new research proves the opposite.

A meta-analytic review of over eight hundred teams shows that individuals are more likely to generate a higher number of original ideas when they don't interact with others.[32] The push for hyper-collaboration drains people, creating collaboration burnout that undermines performance as much as it enhances it.

Research by Morten T. Hansen, professor of management at UC Berkeley, reveals how leaders' obsession with collaboration can quickly destroy value.[33] As Hansen explains: "Too often a business leader asks, 'How can we get people to collaborate more?' That's the wrong question. It should be, 'Will collaboration on this project create or destroy value?'"

Yet executives keep expecting teams to collaborate without designing the conditions that make it possible. As Fredrik Nael puts it: "It takes both sides to build a bridge." But leaders expect teams to build bridges while standing on opposite sides of a canyon.

The collaboration obsession can be harmful in several ways:

- **Being "always on":** Organizations expect people to be constantly available and connected. Teams jump from meetings to online chats to group projects without time for deep, focused work. This leads to burnout, with employees spending more time and effort on coordinating than on actually working.
- **Seeking consensus:** Leaders think good collaboration means everyone getting along and agreeing. They confuse working together with reaching consensus. This makes healthy disagreement seem like a problem rather than a valuable part of teamwork.
- **Forcing teamwork:** Return-to-office mandates are a good example of this. Despite evidence showing the benefits of deep work and asynchronous collaboration, companies push for everyone to be together. They wrongly assume that more togetherness automatically means better results.

Even worse, many leaders think collaboration happens automatically rather than it being a skill they need to develop. They assemble an all-star team and expect them to work well together. But research by Dr. Heidi Gardner shows this approach doesn't work:[34] Simply putting experts on the same project isn't enough—leaders must create the right conditions for collaboration to happen.

Why Collaboration Really Fails

Collaboration fails not because people resist working together, but because asking for help often feels risky or shameful.

The cult of collaboration obscures this simple truth. While we created complex frameworks around teamwork, we ignored a fundamental truth: Effective collaboration happens when people feel comfortable seeking help.

Yet most workplace cultures undermine this reality. Asking for help is seen as weakness. It's unclear whom to approach, how trust must be earned, or what the decision-making processes are. No wonder meetings are unproductive and cross-functional projects stall.

What's often overlooked is how leaders fail to design for collaboration. Putting people on a team together or establishing KPIs isn't enough. Leaders must intentionally create norms and structure to help their teams succeed.

In my experience, collaboration breaks down because of four main traps:

1. **Overconfidence:** People don't realize they need help.
2. **Self-reliance:** Even when they do realize they need help, people are reluctant to ask for it.
3. **Low trust:** People don't believe others will follow through.
4. **Unclear decision-making:** No one knows who owns what.

Let's examine each barrier.

Barrier 1: The Overconfidence Trap

People often struggle to recognize when they need help. Experience, while valuable, can create a false sense of confidence that blinds us to our limitations. Over time, successful people may rely too heavily on instinct and dismiss the value of other perspectives.

Research shows that experienced managers tend to overestimate their leadership effectiveness more than junior managers do.[35] Another study found that most senior leaders often rate their skills and expertise more highly than their colleagues do.

This overconfidence prevents teams from seeking input that could improve outcomes, leaving them working with incomplete information.

Barrier 2: The Self-Reliance Trap

Even when people know they need help, asking for it means overcoming pride in a culture that celebrates independence. As sociologist Wayne Baker observed, "In many Western cultures, we have a strong value of self-reliance and individualism that gets in the way of asking for what we need."[36]

Organizations expect people to have all the answers, which contradicts human nature. We're inherently imperfect, often unsure, and regularly need support. This fundamental contradiction—rewarding self-sufficiency while demanding collaboration—keeps people isolated just when they should be connecting.

Barrier 3: The Low Trust Trap

The third barrier to collaboration is lack of trust in those who could help you. Effective collaboration depends on what I call the Three Pillars of Trust:

1. **Competence:** believing others have the skills to help
2. **Caring:** believing they have your best interests at heart

3. **Consistency:** believing they'll follow through on commitments and what they say

Research by Paul J. Zak found that high-trust teams report better collaboration and productivity.[37] Without all three pillars, people may go through the motions of collaboration but withhold real engagement. True trust determines whether collaboration feels safe, meaningful, and worth the risk.

Barrier 4: The Unclear Decision-Making Trap

Perhaps the most damaging barrier to collaboration is confusion about how decisions get made. Advisors assume they're shaping decisions when they're only informing them. Subject matter experts are brought in too late into the process to make an impact. Decision-makers think everyone is aligned while teams quietly disagree.

Some people treat decisions as final, while others assume they're still up for discussion. The result? Endless revisiting and stalled progress. As McKinsey reports, only one in five executives says their organization excels at decision-making.[38]

What derails progress isn't disagreement—it's ambiguity. Without clear roles and defined decision rules, teams lose momentum. People don't know whom to ask for help, who has authority, or when a decision is final. When that clarity is missing, collaboration becomes confusing and frustrating.

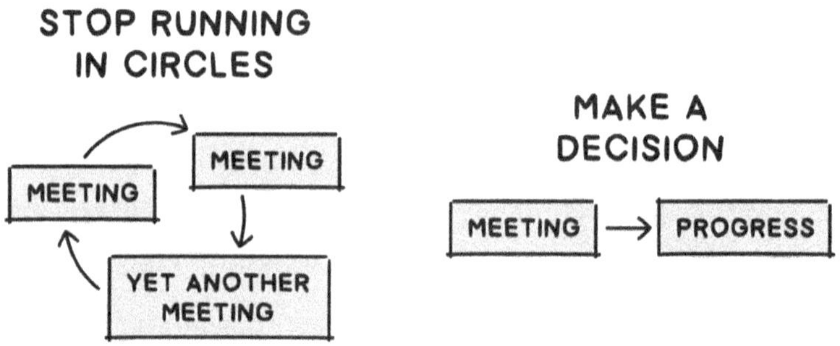

STOP RUNNING IN CIRCLES

MEETING
MEETING
YET ANOTHER MEETING

MAKE A DECISION

MEETING → PROGRESS

How Collaboration Debt Drives Backward Talk

Left unresolved, collaboration debt doesn't just slow teams down—it stalls their conversations. Instead of surfacing issues directly, teams fall into Backward Talk.

These patterns often show up in two forms:

- **Primary pattern: blame.** When collaborative efforts fail, teams reflexively look for culprits rather than solutions:
  - "Marketing never gave us clear requirements."
  - "If engineering had been in the loop earlier, this wouldn't have happened."
  - "The executive team keeps changing priorities."

Blame provides comfort—it removes agency by pointing the finger at someone else instead of examining what we could do differently. Finding a scapegoat is easier than addressing the uncomfortable truth: Our collaborative processes need improvement.

- **Secondary pattern: avoidance.** After blame cycles damage relationships and trust, teams start sidestepping real issues entirely:
  - "Let's schedule another meeting to continue this discussion."

- "We need more stakeholder input before we can decide."
- "Let's table this for now and revisit next quarter."

These patterns merely create an illusion of progress, preventing teams from addressing core collaboration challenges.

How Collaboration Debt Manifests

Collaboration debt doesn't announce itself with dramatic team meltdowns. It shows up in the grinding frustration of teams that talk endlessly but decide nothing.

Here are the most common ways collaboration debt reveals itself:

- **The "we" that means nobody:** "We'll take care of this" instead of "Michelle will own this and complete it by Friday." This diluted ownership language feels inclusive but prevents accountability.
- **Collaboration theater:** Teams perform the rituals of collaboration without the substance required. They hold elaborate input-gathering sessions, cross-functional workshops, and alignment meetings that produce no actual decisions or progress.
- **Help avoidance:** Despite preaching collaboration, people resist asking for assistance because it feels like admitting weakness. Teams suffer in silence rather than leverage collective expertise.
- **"Workslop":** People dump AI-generated content or proposals on their team without properly vetting them. This creates extra work for their colleagues who have to fix it. The person

who generated the content thinks they're being productive. The person cleaning it up thinks their coworker is lazy.[39]

- **Consensus paralysis:** Teams confuse collaboration with unanimous agreement, meaning they spend endless time trying to get everyone to support every decision rather than making clear choices and moving forward.

The most revealing diagnostic? Team members can't clearly answer questions like, "Who owns this decision?" or "When will this be resolved?" Answers like those mean you're witnessing collaboration debt in action.

Here's how collaboration debt compares to healthy collaboration:

Collaboration Debt	Healthy Collaboration
Everyone's accountable, so no one truly is	Collective ownership and individual accountability
Decision-making limbo	Clear decision-making rights and roles
Asking for help feels like admitting weakness	People ask for help when they need it
Trust is earned, not assumed	Trust is assumed through competence, caring, and consistency
Everyone must have input on everything	The right people are involved at the right time; others remain informed
More time spent coordinating than actually working	Protected focus time with intentional check-ins

Canceling Collaboration Debt: GM's Cultural Reset

When Mary Barra was promoted to CEO of General Motors in 2014, the company was facing serious collaboration problems. Teams were stuck in decision-making limbo, and only cared about their departments. A recent safety crisis had exposed how bad news traveled slowly, accountability was diffused, and departments operated in silos.

The company's dress code illustrated this dysfunction: ten pages of rules that treated managers like children while expecting them to make million-dollar decisions. The real issue wasn't the policy but what it represented. It taught teams to wait for permission instead of taking ownership.

Rather than writing better policies, GM's leadership made a simple choice: trust people to think for themselves.[40] The dress code became just two words: "Dress appropriately." When managers asked for details, they got a clear answer: "You're accountable for leading your team."

This approach was applied to other policies later, including remote work ("Work appropriately"). The goal was to build a culture of ownership.

GM also started promoting "Seek truth," a motto to encourage intellectual honesty and better decision-making. Employees were expected to provide the complete picture, supported with data—even when it was uncomfortable. This stopped siloed solutions and encouraged company-wide thinking. Teams stopped protecting their departments and started solving problems together.

GM had suffered from years of bad choices based on assumptions, office politics, and selfish interests. This transformation created more open debates, where honesty mattered more than being right. A truth-telling culture also accelerated innovation by making it okay to challenge the status quo. Barra said it best: "It's OK to admit what you don't know. It's OK to ask for help. And it's more than OK to listen to the people you lead. In fact, it's essential."

The "Seek truth" approach transformed GM's culture. Teams that had wasted months in meetings suddenly had clear authority to act. The company once known for committee culture became known for open conversations and decisive action.

Spotting Your Collaboration Debt

Use the following questions to assess where collaboration may be holding your team back. Treat them as prompts for honest reflection, not for perfect answers.

Decision-Making

- Are people clear on how decisions are made and who has the authority to make them?
- Do teams make decisions efficiently, without endless rounds of input-gathering?
- Are those closest to the problem empowered to make the call?

Meetings

- Do your meetings consistently produce clear outcomes and next steps?
- Are meeting participants limited to those who can actually contribute to the decision?
- Do people leave meetings energized about what they're going to accomplish?

Norms and Rules

- Do your collaboration processes help work get done, rather than create bureaucratic overhead?
- Are conflicts addressed directly through conversation, rather than avoided through new rules?
- Do people know how to escalate issues without creating bottlenecks?

Coordination and Flow

- Does important information reach the right people without overwhelming everyone else?
- Can individuals focus on deep work without constant coordination interruptions?
- Do handoffs between team members happen smoothly, with clear expectations?

With our cultish insistence on collaboration, we're harming our ability to get work done. Teams now spend more energy coordinating than executing, confusing endless input-gathering with actual progress. Real collaboration isn't about including everyone in everything—it's about intentional coordination that amplifies individual strengths while maintaining focus on outcomes.

Once you've identified the areas where collaboration debt is holding your team back, you can begin to make targeted changes that restore clarity, trust, and momentum.

In the next chapter, we'll explore how you can strategically tackle the debt costing you and your team the most.

CHAPTER 11

Manage Your Conversational Debt

"The best time to plant a tree was twenty years ago. The second-best time is now."

—Chinese Proverb

Now it's time to deal with our conversational debt.

Picture this: You finally work up the courage to spread out all your credit card statements, bank notices, and loan documents across your kitchen table. The numbers stare back at you—some worse than expected, others surprisingly manageable. That sick feeling in your stomach? It's not just seeing the debt: It's realizing you've been avoiding this moment for weeks or months, while the interest has just kept compounding.

But here's the thing: Laying everything out is also the first step toward freedom. After all, you can't manage what you can't see.

Now comes the harder question: What do you tackle first?

Just as financial advisors help you prioritize which debts to pay first, you need a strategic approach to address previously avoided conversations.

Not all unaddressed conversations are created equal. Some require minimal effort yet produce substantial benefits. Others represent expensive sunk costs, where the opportunity for productive resolution has already passed.

The temptation is to tackle everything at once or avoid the whole mess entirely. Both approaches fail. Strategic debt management means making deliberate choices about which conversations to have, when to have them, and—just as importantly—which ones to let go.

The irony isn't lost on me that we are speaking of debt here in Chapter 11. In the United States, Chapter 11 is the *bankruptcy code* that lets companies restructure their debt to avoid going under. Consider this your conversational debt reorganization plan.

In this chapter, we'll explore how to develop a strategic path forward. You'll learn how to assess the conversations your team has been avoiding—based on impact, urgency, effort, and relevance.

Understanding Your Debt Profile

To break the pattern of conversational debt, you need to understand which psychological traps are driving your team's specific debt patterns so you can choose the right way to address them.

Use this table to identify which trap is driving your team's patterns, then focus on the specific shift needed.

	Alignment	Belonging	Collaboration
The Psychology	Alignment Trap—It's easier to assume we're aligned than realize we're not. We sidestep clarifying real alignment because it might reveal uncomfortable differences.	Tyranny of Harmony—We go along to belong to the group/tribe. Group harmony matters more than individual truth.	Teamwork Obsession—When things don't go as planned, we blame a colleague, or other departments or teams.
Primary Backward Talk Pattern	**Avoidance**	**Groupthink**	**Blame**
Secondary Backward Talk Pattern	Groupthink	Avoidance	Avoidance
Shift Needed	Stop assuming people are aligned. Address misalignment directly to surface dissent.	Stop going along with artificial consensus. Challenge groupthink, even if it creates tension.	Stop blaming others for systemic issues. Focus on improving the system—and your role.

Understanding your team's debt profile helps you move beyond generic solutions. In the next section, we'll walk through four strategic approaches to debt management and show you how to match each one to the realities of your debt profile.

Four Strategic Approaches to Debt Management

Behavioral economics research on temporal discounting reveals why we systematically undervalue future benefits relative to immediate rewards.[41] This also explains why teams accumulate conversational debt despite knowing better.

Strategic debt management is about reversing that bias. It works by making future costs visible and reducing the friction of action in the present.

The reality is, we aren't naturally wired for optimal debt management. Rather, we need systems and strategies that work *with* our psychological tendencies, not *against* them.

In the next section, you'll learn four distinct approaches—Flurry, Snowball, Avalanche, and Drift—to help you prioritize conversations based on your team's capacity, your debt profile, and where progress is most likely. Each strategy is illustrated with a real-life example from my work helping teams break these patterns, and connects to the Conversational Debt Canvas that we'll explore more in Chapter 12.

1. The Flurry Approach: Start with Quick Wins

The Flurry approach builds early momentum by focusing on easy conversations that require minimal effort—the "low-hanging fruit" of conversational debt.

Quick wins matter. They generate forward movement, boost team spirit, and build the confidence for tackling harder issues later.

Case Study: Every sprint planning meeting at this tech company felt like Groundhog Day. Every week, the product team would circle the same questions: Who makes the final call? Whose input matters? Without clear decision ownership, meetings dragged on, and everyone felt frustrated.

The solution was surprisingly simple: I facilitated a short workshop to clarify decision-making processes and roles.

The team made three key agreements:

- **Decision owner:** The product manager gets to make the final call on features, but must consult engineering on feasibility first.
- **Input limits:** A maximum of four voices are allowed per decision—more becomes coordination theater.
- **Time boundaries:** All input must be gathered within one week, with a decision made by the following Monday.

The Result: Immediate improvement. The team saved hours each week and got more work done.

When to Use This Approach:

- You're new to addressing conversational debt.
- Morale or trust needs a boost.
- You need early, visible progress.

Canvas Signal: Look for scattered avoidance patterns and minor collaboration debts like repeated "unclear decisions"—problems that are annoying but not deeply systemic.

Why It Works: Success breeds success. Each resolved conversation builds evidence that difficult topics are survivable and valuable.

2. The Snowball Approach: Build Momentum

This approach builds on early wins to tackle bigger issues. Success with one conversation builds confidence for the next, creating positive effects across different debt types.

This strategy leverages a behavioral insight called *mental accounting*—our tendency to treat things in separate "buckets" rather than as part of a whole. Teams often fall into this trap with conversations, treating belonging issues, collaboration breakdowns, and alignment problems as unrelated when they're actually deeply connected.

The Snowball approach tackles underlying problems first to create lasting momentum.

Case Study: A global consulting firm was suffering from chronic meeting dysfunction: too many participants, unclear roles, and hours of discussion with no resolution.

To fix the issue, leaders imposed a rule: No more than six people per meeting. But this backfired. Team members felt left out, complaining about missing important decisions.

Digging deeper, I found the real issue wasn't about meetings but about belonging. In this company, a meeting invite signaled that you mattered.

To move forward, we had to reframe visibility. We created other ways for people to contribute and stay informed without attending every meeting. Once people felt valued regardless of being invited or not, the smaller meetings finally worked.

The Result: Smaller, more effective meetings and a broader culture shift toward valuing contribution over mere presence.

When to Use This Approach:

- You want to build capacity progressively.
- Success in one area could help another.
- Your team is ready to move beyond quick wins.

Canvas Signal: Connected patterns across multiple debt types, especially when one type (like belonging) is clearly fueling the others.

Why It Works: Confidence spreads. Teams that handle one tough conversation well develop the muscle for the next. Each success lays the groundwork for tackling bigger issues.

3. The Avalanche Approach: Tackle the Biggest Problem First

The Avalanche approach targets your most important debt first—no matter how hard it is to solve. It's named after the financial strategy of paying off the most expensive debt before tackling smaller ones, even though it takes more effort.

This works best when a single unresolved issue is creating ripple effects across your team. It requires courage, clarity, and often external facilitation, but the payoff is immediate and far-reaching.

Case Study: A healthcare startup had been stuck for over a year because of a fundamental disagreement. The CEO wanted rapid, VC-funded growth while medical leadership advocated for sustainable, values-based scaling.

This misalignment affected everything—hiring, product development, weekly priorities, and team dynamics.

Finally, the leadership team committed to a three-day offsite to address the issue head-on. It wasn't easy. Tensions ran high, and the stakes were real. Though extremely difficult—one of the toughest offsites I've facilitated—it proved transformational.

By the end of the session, they'd made key decisions together instead of delaying further for weeks.

The Result: Clear direction replaced uncertainty. Trust began to rebuild. And the organization moved forward with renewed focus and better decision-making.

When to Use This Approach:

- One major issue is blocking everything else.
- Your team faces time pressure, has strong trust, or has external support (e.g., a facilitator).
- You're ready for deep, focused work.

Canvas Signal: Look for one dominant debt type overshadowing others, or a core issue sitting at the intersection of alignment, belonging, and collaboration.

Why It Works: Big problems don't fix themselves. You must address them head-on.

4. The Drift Approach: Strategic Letting Go

Like snowdrifts that eventually melt on their own, some issues lose importance over time. Not every problem is worth solving. The Drift approach recognizes when it's better to let go of certain issues—not by avoiding them, but by making a deliberate choice to disengage with them.

This approach helps teams avoid the sunk-cost fallacy: continuing to invest in something just because you've already put so much into it.

Case Study: A leadership team at a consumer goods company held on to resentment over a poor hiring decision. During a crisis, the CEO had appointed a CFO who ultimately proved ineffective, and it took too long to replace him.

When we finally discussed the issue, the context had changed. The new CFO was performing exceptionally. The company was thriving. Yet the emotional scars remained.

The team had two choices: Rehash the old mistake or focus on the present.

They chose to acknowledge the frustration, learn from it, and move forward—without reopening old wounds. This wasn't about denial, but about strategic letting-go.

The Result: A renewed focus on current priorities, and a shared understanding that some issues require release, not resolution.

When to Use This Approach:

- Old grievances no longer matter.
- Relationships are damaged beyond repair.
- Teams are temporarily or permanently disbanded.
- Decisions can't be reversed.

Canvas Signal: Look for legacy issues from former team members, outdated business contexts, or debt clusters tied to irreversible decisions.

Why It Works: Sometimes the smartest move is letting go. Not every conversation needs closure—some just need to be put to rest.

Each of the four approaches has its place in conversational debt management. The key is making deliberate choices about which debts to address and how, rather than allowing debt to accumulate blindly, hoping it will somehow resolve itself.

From Conversational Debt to Freedom

By now, you should have a better understanding of how conversational debt accumulates across three dimensions—alignment, belonging, and collaboration—and how these debts feed one another in destructive spirals. You also have four strategic debt management approaches (Flurry, Snowball, Avalanche, Drift) for prioritizing which conversations to tackle first.

In the next chapter, you'll map where exactly you're stuck, and how to move from Backward Talk patterns into Forward Talk progress.

CHAPTER 12

Map Your Conversational Debt

By now, you've seen how conversational debt builds—often invisibly—across meetings, messages, and misaligned assumptions. You've explored how alignment, belonging, and collaboration debts feed one another, creating spirals that trap even smart teams in destructive patterns.

Now comes the critical question: Where, exactly, is your team stuck?

Remember the conversational roundabout from Chapter 6? Teams get stuck circling the same conversations—taking the wrong exits, unable to find their way forward. When conversational debt accumulates, a simple roundabout can start to feel like a destructive tornado. That's why I created the Conversational Debt Spiral Canvas, a visual tool to help your team see exactly where they're caught and how to chart their escape route.

Conversational Debt Spiral©

Identify communication breakdowns before the damage compounds

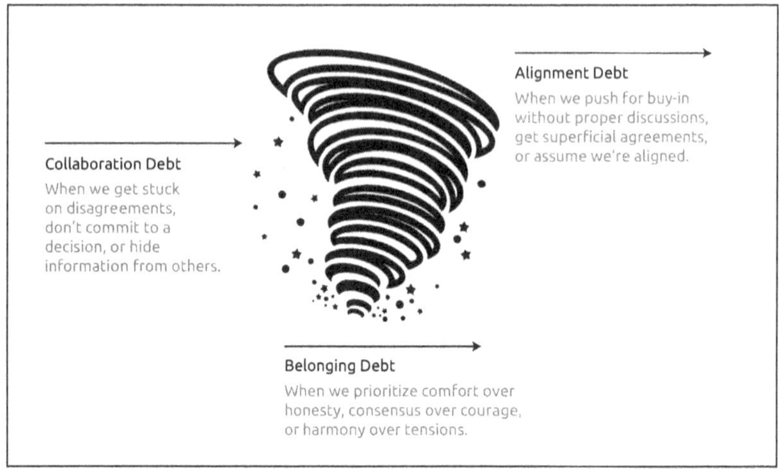

Each type of debt—alignment, belonging, and collaboration—acts like a separate atmospheric pressure system feeding the vortex. When the debts converge, they create a force that pulls teams deeper into Backward Talk patterns until they're caught in a cycle they can't escape.

How the Debt Spiral Forms

These three debts don't operate independently—they feed into one another, creating an increasingly powerful downward spiral.

Poor alignment creates unclear expectations, leading people to avoid difficult clarifying conversations (belonging debt), which results in endless circular discussions without resolution (collaboration debt).

Artificial harmony prevents teams from surfacing different interpretations of decisions (alignment debt), making it impossible to have the productive conflict needed for real collaboration (collaboration debt).

Process dysfunction makes it harder for people to feel heard and valued (belonging debt) and prevents the clear decisions needed for genuine alignment (alignment debt).

The math is brutal: As conversational debt compounds, each type makes the others worse, pulling teams deeper into the vortex until they can barely function.

Let's go through a quick recap of the three debts before we explore how to use the canvas:

Alignment debt occurs when teams confuse nodding heads with genuine commitment. Everyone appears to agree in meetings, but people leave with fundamentally different interpretations of decisions, priorities, and next steps.

Belonging debt accumulates when teams prioritize artificial harmony over authentic dialogue. People withhold concerns, soften feedback, and avoid challenging popular ideas to maintain group cohesion.

Collaboration debt builds when teams fail to reach a resolution. Decisions are never final, meetings end by scheduling another meeting, and simple disagreements transform into endless discussions. Teams get stuck debating who has decision authority while opportunities slip away.

Using the Canvas for Debt Diagnosis

Step 1: Set the Stage

Establish the purpose: This conversation can happen between leaders or with the entire team present. While you don't necessarily need an offsite, you must carve out a couple of uninterrupted hours to have meaningful conversations. The goal is understanding, not fixing everything immediately. Think of it as installing a radar system for conversational debt.

Step 2: Map the Type of Debt

Have everyone silently identify specific examples where each type of debt shows up:

Alignment Debt: "Where do we think we agree but actually don't?" (*The pricing strategy that everyone "supports" but interprets differently.*)

- Where do we confuse agreement with true commitment?
- What decisions do we interpret completely differently?
- When do we rush to agree without ensuring shared understanding?

Belonging Debt: "What do we avoid saying to keep the peace?" (*We avoided giving feedback for months, then exploded with built-up frustration over something small.*)

- When do we hold back perspectives to avoid being difficult?
- Where do we silence concerns to maintain consensus?
- What conversations do we avoid by protecting team harmony?

Collaboration Debt: "Where do we talk in circles without deciding?" (*The workflow improvement has been "under discussion" for three months.*)

- Where do we delay decisions or avoid pushing for closure?
- What information silos slow us down?
- What conversations keep circling without clear next steps?

Focus on real examples—not hypotheticals—in the appropriate sections, clustering similar items.

Step 3: Reflect on the Impact

For each cluster, assess the damage:

- How long has this been pulling us down?
- What's the real cost of staying caught in this pattern?
- How does this debt make the other types worse?

Encourage people to notice overlaps—debt types often reinforce one another and compound the spiral.

Step 4: Identify Your Escape Route

You can't fix everything at once. Trying to address all debt simultaneously often just makes the vortex stronger. Use strategic prioritization:

- Which debt is growing fastest, creating the most downward pull?
- Which would be easiest to address first to weaken the overall vortex?
- Which has the biggest impact on your team's ability to function?

Select one to two specific debts as your primary escape focus.

Step 5: Plan Your Escape

For each debt you choose to address, reflect on the following:

- What specific conversation needs to happen to reduce this debt?
- Who must be involved to make it stick?
- When and where will you attempt this conversation?
- What would success look like? How will you know the debt is decreasing?

Setting clear milestones drives momentum. When team members commit to clear actions, they stop getting stuck and start moving forward.

Use the table below to guide your choices:

If your canvas reveals	Start with this approach	Why this works
Multiple minor issues scattered across debt types	**Flurry approach**	Builds momentum and confidence through quick wins before tackling systemic issues
Belonging debt feeding into collaboration problems	**Snowball approach**	Early wins with strengthening team trust can improve decision-making conversations
One major alignment issue driving most other problems	**Avalanche approach**	Addresses the root cause, creating cascading effects across all team interactions
Historical grievances mixed with current issues	**Drift approach** for outdated problems	Lets you focus energy on current issues that can actually be resolved

The conversations you mapped in your canvas aren't going away on their own. They're accumulating interest on problems you'll eventually have to address.

Act now.

But all the diagnosis and strategy in the world won't help if people lack the courage to have those difficult conversations.

The real barrier to Forward Talk isn't just knowing what needs to be said—it's finding the individual and collective courage to say it when it matters most. That's exactly what we'll tackle in Part III.

PART II RECAP

Break Free from Debt

In Summary:

Conversational debt accumulates when teams confuse motion with progress. Three types of debt feed one another: alignment debt (We agreed but meant different things), belonging debt (We stay quiet to keep the peace), and collaboration debt (We keep having meetings but nothing gets resolved).

Start by mapping where the debt is growing faster. Prioritize which conversations to tackle first, which to have later, and which to drop.

Key Takeaways:

- Break the pattern. Regret comes from silence, not action.
- Overcommunication doesn't fix alignment issues, just like being nice doesn't make up for not being honest.
- When we avoid a conversation, don't just put off discomfort. We damage trust.
- Collaboration requires friction and commitment. Encourage debate, but make sure you reach resolution.
- Pick your battles. Use quick wins to build momentum. Save deeper interventions for critical issues. Know when to let go.

Before You Finish

You now know how to spot what's stopping your team from having better conversations—and how to fix it.

Ready to use Forward Talk with your team? Start here:

- Take the quiz to identify your team's conversational debt
- Use the templates to surface difficult topics
- Check the resources to choose where to start

Go to gustavorazzetti.com/forward-talk-tools
or scan the QR code below.

PART III

Reclaim Your Voice

CHAPTER 13

Regain Conversational Agency

"When the whole world is silent, even one voice becomes powerful."

—Malala Yousafzai

Every day, teams are giving away their power without even noticing it.

In meeting rooms across every industry, smart people are making costly choices. Faced with the discomfort of taking responsibility for uncertain outcomes, they surrender their agency to someone else. They blame others instead of examining the systems in place. They defer to group consensus instead of trusting their own perspectives. They wait for someone else to speak up first.

This isn't cowardice—it's a rational response to an irrational situation. It's easier to point fingers, follow the crowd, and hope someone else will handle the hard stuff. But taking back your agency means sharing your thoughts, even if you might be wrong or if others reject your ideas.

This rejection is hard enough, but my research has revealed that not speaking up kicks off an even more challenging cycle: When people feel hopeless about change, they're actually experiencing something deeper—they feel powerless because they've surrendered their voice. It turns out that, in trying to avoid discomfort, we've become our worst enemy.

Here's how this surrender happens:

When we choose avoidance, we surrender our voices to silence, hoping someone else will speak up—or, worse, that issues will magically disappear.

When we default to blame, we surrender our power to cosmic justice, focusing on past mistakes instead of what we can learn or do about them.

When we fall into groupthink, we surrender our judgment to social pressure, trusting what the majority thinks over our own view of reality.

Forward Talk is the antidote. Instead of surrendering to Backward Talk patterns, we intentionally own our voice and our part of the conversation.

In Part II, you learned about the symptoms—how conversational debt accumulates when teams avoid difficult conversations. Now we're going to the root cause: why smart people systematically give away the very capabilities that would prevent that debt from building up in the first place.

The three patterns below aren't just communication problems—they are power transfers. Each time you choose avoidance over voice, blame over ownership, or groupthink over independent judgment, you're making a trade: temporary comfort for long-term agency.

Understanding exactly how you surrender your power is the first step to reclaiming it.

Three Ways We Surrender Our Power

Let's explore how these patterns manifest—and why we've become accustomed to them, even if they cost us dearly.

1. Avoidance: Why Silence Makes Everything Worse

In 1964, Kitty Genovese was murdered outside her apartment in Queens. Two weeks later, *The New York Times* reported that thirty-seven neighbors had witnessed the attack, but no one had intervened or called the police.[42] While the media greatly exaggerated the number of passive witnesses, the story became a symbol of apathy that inspired psychologists John Darley and Bibb Latané to investigate human *inaction*.

In Darley and Latané's experiments,[43] students believed they were participating in a group discussion over an intercom when one person appeared to have a seizure. When participants thought they were the only witnesses, 85 percent reported the emergency. However, when they believed others had also observed the seizure, that number dropped to just 31 percent.

This became known as the "Bystander Effect": The more people who are present at an emergency, the less likely we are to intervene. But here's what's crucial—it's not just the presence of others that causes inaction but the diffusion of responsibility. When everyone is responsible, we feel less compelled to act.

We don't stay silent because we're scared. Rather, we stay quiet because we surrender our responsibility to others.

This same dynamic plays out in teams every day. For example, a client relationship may be deteriorating, and the complaints keep coming, but no one wants to address the real issue. Everyone stays silent, waiting for someone else to speak up. Three months later, the client terminates the contract. The exit interview reveals specific steps that could have turned things around, but it's too late to do anything about it.

Avoidance feels like prudence, but it's actually paralysis disguised as patience. We convince ourselves that waiting is wisdom, when it's really surrender.

We focus on the risks of taking action instead of the costs of inaction. We imagine perfect future conversations led by braver people with better timing, better authority, and better information. Meanwhile, the opportunity to fix things slips away.

When we surrender our responsibility, we don't just lose our voice—we become invisible.

And invisible people can't address real issues or move toward solutions.

2. Blame: Finding Fault Fixes Nothing

Just four days after the sinking of the RMS *Titanic* in the early hours of April 15, 1912, a rushed inquiry was convened in New York. Another would follow in Britain in May. They concluded that the White Star Line was not guilty of negligence.[44] And, although the shipping company would be taken to court and ordered to pay out, the fines weren't huge.

Even though the *Titanic*'s fatally inadequate number of lifeboats caused countless deaths, the shipping company got a pass. The inquiries concluded that no rules were broken—simply because existing regulations were outdated. That verdict conveniently protected the company.

However, people were thirsty for blood, so the blame shifted elsewhere. The greatest ire was reserved for the SS *Californian* and its captain, Stanley Lord, who allegedly ignored distress signals from the *Titanic*. The accusations destroyed Captain Lord's reputation. It wasn't until decades later that the discovery of the *Titanic*'s wreck exonerated both Lord and the SS *Californian*'s role in the disaster.[45]

The pattern is as ancient as it is predictable: When disaster strikes, we look for someone to blame rather than what to fix in ourselves or our organization. Blame gives us the illusion that cosmic justice—the universal balance of fairness—has been served, even when the underlying problems remain unchanged.

This isn't just tradition—blame works as a coping mechanism, and modern psychology explains why this feels so satisfying. When we mess up, we experience internal tension: Even though we're a good person, we've made a mistake. The brain resolves this conflict by blaming external factors such as our colleagues, market conditions, or flawed data. Blame puts us back in the driver's seat.

Psychologist Jennifer Lerner found that people are more likely to assign blame when they feel angry rather than sad.[46] Anger triggers a desire to find a culprit. Sadness, on the other hand, prompts reflection. In team environments, blame spirals outward, morphing into "us vs. them" narratives.

Blame feels like moral clarity, but it's really moral abdication. By pointing fingers at others, we make a devastating trade: We exchange the discomfort of self-reflection for the comfort of clean villains and victims.

Pointing fingers feels like taking action, but it's a way of surrendering our power to the illusion of cosmic justice.

Teams often fall into this trap and play the blame game. A software release fails spectacularly, customer complaints flood in, and management calls for a post-mortem. Within minutes, the team identifies the culprit: the QA engineer who missed the critical bug.

Case closed. Justice served. Cosmic order restored.

Except nothing actually improves.

Instead of focusing on what we can control—our response, the processes, and the lessons learned—we focus on what we can't control: other people's characters. We exchange responsibility for fixing systems for the punishment of individuals. Every minute spent finding fault is a minute not spent building solutions.

When we surrender our power to cosmic justice, we don't just avoid solutions; we become powerless. And powerless people get stuck relitigating the past instead of building the future.

3. Groupthink: When Agreeing Makes Us Dumber

A college student walked into what he believed was a simple vision test at Swarthmore College in 1951. The task seemed embarrassingly easy: Match the length of one line to three comparison lines. The answer was obvious—as clear as the difference between a pencil and a ruler.

But when all the other students gave the same obviously wrong answer, he changed his mind and joined them. He chose social acceptance over the evidence of his own eyes.

This student had unknowingly become part of Solomon Asch's famous psychology experiment.[47] The other "students" were actors, pretending to be participants in the study about how social pressure influences judgment. In the end, 75 percent of real participants conformed at least once, choosing the incorrect answer just to go along with the group.

Psychologist Irving Janis expanded on this idea by analyzing historical failures, including the Bay of Pigs invasion. His research led to the term *groupthink*—the tendency for teams to prioritize cohesion and agreement over critical thinking.[48] In 1960, US President John F. Kennedy's advisors failed to challenge the flawed plan to invade Cuba. The desire to maintain unity suppressed dissent, ultimately leading to a catastrophic decision.

We often betray our reality to please others, surrendering our judgment to social pressure.

This shows up in teams all the time. In one example, a marketing team unanimously approved a campaign targeting millennials. Six months later, the campaign flopped. In the post-mortem, it emerged that several team members had had serious concerns about the messaging. Even the creative director had admitted privately that he felt it was off-brand. But no one spoke up.

Groupthink often masquerades as harmony, but it's really consensus disguising disagreement. We trade personal expertise and direct observations for the illusion of group wisdom. Even when the evidence says otherwise, we defer to what others seem to believe.

When we surrender our judgment to social pressure, we don't just risk poor decisions—we begin to doubt our own reality.

And people who doubt their reality settle for average solutions.

These three Backward Talk patterns—avoidance, blame, and groupthink—all represent a form of surrender of power. The table below shows what we give up in each case, the belief that fuels it, and the courageous response that moves us into Forward Talk.

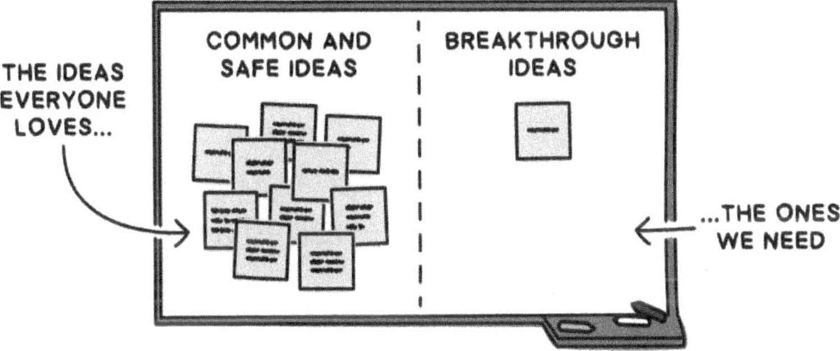

How We Surrender Our Power

Backward Talk	AVOIDANCE	BLAME	GROUPTHINK
What We Surrender	Responsibility to others/future	Power to "cosmic justice"	Judgment to social pressure
Psychological State	INVISIBLE	POWERLESS	DOUBTFUL
Core Belief	"Someone else will handle it."	"If we find the villain, order will be restored."	"The group agrees, so I must be wrong."
Forward Talk Response	**VOICE** Courage to speak up and take initiative	**OWNERSHIP** Courage to own your role, responsibility, and mistakes	**CHALLENGE** Courage to trust your reality and question consensus

These patterns reveal precisely how we give away our power in everyday conversations. Recognizing what we're surrendering is the first step toward reclaiming our agency and redirecting the conversation.

When Smart People Give Up Power

It was a sweltering summer day in 1974, and Jerry Harvey was visiting his in-laws in Coleman, Texas. The heat was unbearable. When his father-in-law suddenly suggested driving fifty-three miles to Abilene for dinner, Harvey's heart sank—but he went along with the plan.

The trip was miserable, and they returned home hot and irritated. Then came the twist: Harvey's mother-in-law admitted she had thought Abilene was a terrible idea and would have preferred staying home. Harvey and his wife immediately confessed they hadn't wanted to go either, but they'd agreed to keep the peace when everyone else seemed enthusiastic. Even Harvey's father-in-law admitted he never wanted to make the trip in a car without any air conditioning. He'd only suggested it because he thought everyone else was bored.

Harvey coined this dynamic the Abilene Paradox:[49] not a failure to manage conflict, but rather a failure to manage agreement.

When I first heard this story, I had already created the Breaking the Conversational Loop Canvas with its roundabout metaphor. Harvey's family had managed to hit all three Backward Talk patterns in a single afternoon: avoiding conflict, deferring to apparent consensus, and then blaming one another when everything went wrong.

The story illustrates how the three Backward Talk patterns all serve the same psychological function: protecting ourselves from the discomfort of uncertain outcomes.

Blame lets us feel righteous while we surrender our power. *Groupthink* makes us feel safe by surrendering our judgment to collective wisdom. *Avoidance* lets us feel prudent by waiting for perfect conditions.

The Abilene Paradox reveals how surrendering agency traps us in the conversational roundabout. Everyone involved avoided conflict, went along with the consensus, and blamed others when the plan failed. Each surrender made the next easier until they were all miserable in a hot car, heading somewhere nobody wanted to go.

Harvey discovered something that decades of my work with teams has confirmed: Organizations don't just need to handle conflict—they need to accept that disagreement is natural. Rather than rushing to harmony, teams must encourage members to express disagreement. It's easier to commit after authentic debates than after forced silence.

The way out of the roundabout isn't more comfort—it's more courage. Recognizing these patterns is the first step to breaking the cycles, so let's explore how these patterns become contagious and expand across a team.

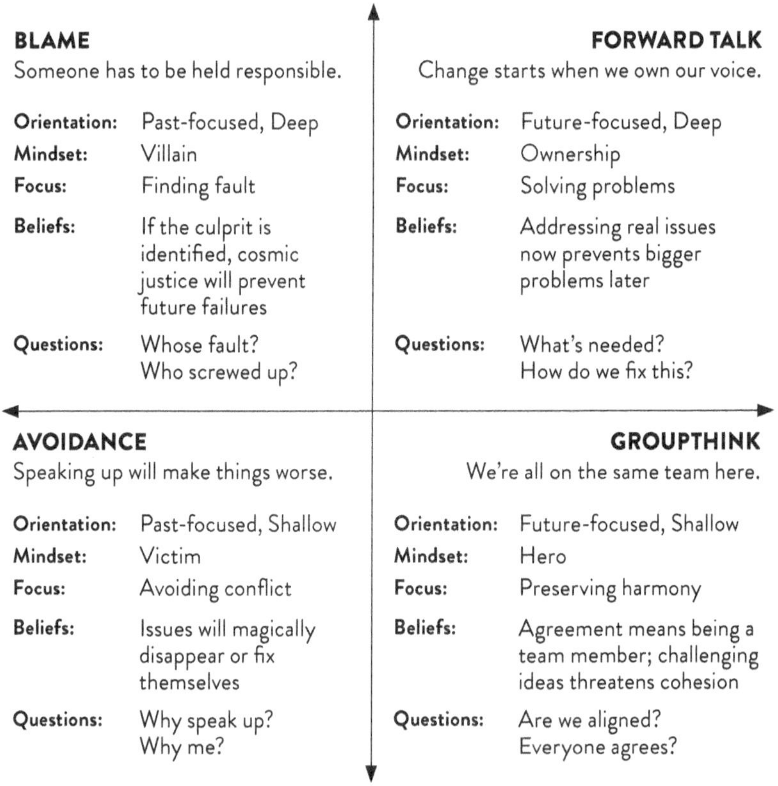

BLAME
Someone has to be held responsible.

Orientation: Past-focused, Deep
Mindset: Villain
Focus: Finding fault
Beliefs: If the culprit is identified, cosmic justice will prevent future failures
Questions: Whose fault? Who screwed up?

FORWARD TALK
Change starts when we own our voice.

Orientation: Future-focused, Deep
Mindset: Ownership
Focus: Solving problems
Beliefs: Addressing real issues now prevents bigger problems later
Questions: What's needed? How do we fix this?

AVOIDANCE
Speaking up will make things worse.

Orientation: Past-focused, Shallow
Mindset: Victim
Focus: Avoiding conflict
Beliefs: Issues will magically disappear or fix themselves
Questions: Why speak up? Why me?

GROUPTHINK
We're all on the same team here.

Orientation: Future-focused, Shallow
Mindset: Hero
Focus: Preserving harmony
Beliefs: Agreement means being a team member; challenging ideas threatens cohesion
Questions: Are we aligned? Everyone agrees?

The Drama Triangle: When Powerlessness Becomes a Team Sport

When you first saw the Forward Talk matrix, you probably thought: *Great model, makes sense, but how does this play out in real conversations?* Here's how.

Every team conversation becomes a stage where people unconsciously audition for three roles that bring those Backward Talk patterns to life. Psychiatrist Stephen Karpman called this the Drama Triangle[50]—and once you see it, it's hard to unsee how teams get trapped in these endless loops.

Meet the cast:

- The Victim avoids real issues by staying stuck in past grievances.
- The Villain blames others while digging deep into what went wrong.
- The Hero rushes toward future solutions without addressing underlying tensions.

Together, they turn every conversation into live theater—and not the good kind.

The triangle creates its own gravitational field. When tensions rise, teams get pulled into these roles without realizing it. Someone becomes the Victim (powerless and blamed), another plays the Villain (blaming and attacking), and another adopts the Hero role (rescuing but controlling).

Each character takes their part too seriously—some even feel virtuous. The Victim feels wronged, the Villain feels righteous, and the Hero feels helpful. But together, they create a system where real solutions become impossible and dysfunction takes over. The Drama Triangle is actually a powerlessness play—and an expensive one.

How Drama Drives Us Backward

Each of these roles corresponds directly to a Backward Talk pattern:

- **Victim → Avoidance:** "Nothing I say matters anyway, so why bother?"
  The Victim surrenders their voice to learned helplessness, waiting for someone else to do something. They avoid speaking up because they've internalized the belief that their input won't change anything.
- **Villain → Blame:** "Someone needs to be held accountable for this mess."
  The Villain surrenders their power to cosmic justice, focusing their energy on finding fault rather than building solutions. They attack problems by attacking people, focusing on where to place blame instead of what needs to be fixed.
- **Hero → Groupthink:** "Let me solve this for everyone so we can all get along."
  The Hero surrenders their judgment to artificial harmony, suppressing dissent and rushing to consensus. They want to impose their solution and save the day.

The cycle is self-reinforcing. Victims add more drama to the fire. Villains respond by doubling down on their attacks. Heroes try to dominate the conversation to silence "negative" voices. Round and round it goes—another conversational roundabout with no exit in sight.

These drama dynamics operate across three levels:

- **Individual:** when someone gets labeled "negative" and becomes the Villain
- **Cultural:** when high-performing cultures reward Hero behaviors, like going "above and beyond"
- **Team:** when leadership makes an unpopular decision and everyone adopts a collective Victim mentality

Regardless of the level, the triangle creates the same outcome: powerlessness disguised as justified roles.

From Drama to Action

The Drama Triangle traps teams in Backward Talk, but here's the breakthrough: Each role contains valuable energy that can be redirected toward Forward Talk. With the right mindset, you can help your team reframe these negative dynamics into positive, powerful ones.

How can you turn the Villain's critical lens into insight instead of discrediting their views? How might Heroes strengthen the team's capacity instead of doing everything themselves? How can Victims refocus their energy into what they can control rather than what they can't?

A few years ago, a sawmill was hemorrhaging $1 million annually due to employee theft. Tools were disappearing at an alarming rate. Workers were taking equipment they didn't even need, turning theft into a company sport. In fact, there was an implicit sense of pride in getting away with it, especially stealing the biggest piece of equipment possible.

Management's first response was a textbook Drama Triangle. They installed surveillance cameras and threatened retaliation. In doing so, they cast employees as potential Villains and themselves as the watchful Heroes. The employees—feeling more victimized than ever—doubled down. The cameras didn't stop the theft; they made the game more exciting.

Then, management brought in organizational psychologist Gary Latham.[51] Instead of playing the Hero and imposing even more control, he did something different: He listened. After interviewing employees, he discovered something that management had missed entirely. The workers weren't stealing for revenge or money. They were stealing for the thrill of it.

Latham's recommendation was counterintuitive: Let employees "borrow" the tools.

The new policy allowed employees to "borrow equipment from the mill anytime they want." The thrill disappeared overnight. Even better, this move reframed the conversation, allowing employees to return previously "borrowed" equipment without retaliation, no questions asked. The theft dropped to almost zero.

This story shows what happens when someone refuses to play their expected role in the Drama Triangle, and chooses a powerful role instead. Rather than being the Hero who swept in with punishment, Latham became a Facilitator who created conditions for a real solution. Instead of treating employees as Villains, he saw them as Challengers to the existing dynamic. Instead of accepting the company's Victim narrative, he helped them become Creators of a new norm.

These three new roles—Challenger, Facilitator, and Creator—are powerful reframes, and instrumental in moving teams from Backward Talk patterns into Forward Talk thinking.

Powerful Role Transformations

When your team slips into the Drama Triangle, you can break the cycle by reframing the roles in real time. Here's how:

Villain → Challenger:

When someone is being dismissive or destructively critical, redirect the focus by saying, "What's the pattern we're trying to change here?"

Key actions:

- Acknowledge their perspective before redirecting.
- Reframe criticism as a question.
- Check if others are noticing the same issue.
- Ask the group: "What else are we missing?"

Challengers reframe issues constructively instead of attacking people. They provide the type of dissent that strengthens decisions rather than destroys relationships. They challenge assumptions to improve outcomes, not to prove others wrong.

Victim → Creator:

When someone focuses on what they can't control or complains about constraints, ask: "What would you need to make progress on this?"

Key actions:

- Ask: "What needs to happen for you to feel supported?"
- Focus on specific requests rather than general complaints.

- Explore: "What can you do with what you have?"
- Seek commitment: "If we get you what you need, what can you commit to achieving?"

Instead of waiting for others to solve their problems, Creators take ownership of what they can control. They focus on desired outcomes rather than dwelling on obstacles. They ask for specific help instead of pity.

Hero → Facilitator:

When someone rushes to impose solutions or force consensus, invite reflection and ask: "What perspectives do we need to hear before we decide?"

Key actions:

- Redirect the focus to gathering input from the right stakeholders.
- Encourage others to share alternative ideas.
- Validate alignment by asking, "What are we not aligned on?"
- Ask: "Who else should weigh in on this?"

Instead of solving everyone's problems, Facilitators create conditions for others to find solutions. They develop team capacity rather than being indispensable. They enable authentic dialogue rather than imposing their ideas.

The Path Forward

We lose power by avoiding difficult conversations. We reclaim it by having them.

The Drama Triangle reveals how teams unconsciously adopt powerless roles: Victims who avoid, Villains who blame, and Heroes who rush to groupthink solutions without resolving tension. However, awareness alone isn't enough. We need to reframe both the roles we play and the conversations we have. Here's how to intentionally regain control of the narrative:

- Instead of avoidance: "Someone has to go first—why not me?"
- Instead of blame, ask: "What's my part in this pattern?"
- Instead of groupthink: "I trust what I'm seeing, even if others don't."

This is Forward Talk in action—not a communication style, but a stance of power and responsibility.

But courage can't stay individual. Social courage must become a shared norm. That means your team must be willing to take social risks together, to share the burden of difficult conversations and create a culture of ownership. High-performing teams refuse to surrender agency—they commit. They own their part, trust their view of reality, and expect everyone to contribute.

The question isn't whether your team will face moments that test their courage. The question is whether they'll reclaim their voice.

In the next chapter, we'll explore how teams can develop the capabilities that make Forward Talk possible. These aren't personality traits that you either have or don't—they're conversational muscles you strengthen through deliberate practice.

CHAPTER 14

From Surrender to Forward Talk

"You can choose courage or you can choose comfort, but you cannot choose both."

—Brené Brown

Manu, a young creative, never imagined his voice could be so powerful until he claimed it without saying a word.

I was sitting in a glass conference room at one of those prestigious ad agencies where an aggressive culture was called "creative passion." The executive creative director—a real bully—had summoned two teams to present their campaign concepts. Everyone knew the drill: Present your work, get demolished, smile, and say, "Thanks for the feedback."

But this time was different. This time was worse.

The director not only attacked everyone's work with his usual arsenal—"This is shit. What were you thinking?"—but he snapped after everyone had finished presenting. He grabbed the carefully crafted pages, ripped them up, and threw them in the air like confetti.

"There," he said, "that's what I think of your *brilliant* ideas."

The room went dead silent. I felt ashamed watching this cruelty. One team member started crying. Weeks of work and late nights now lay scattered on the carpet like evidence of creative murder.

As we were leaving, Manu did something unexpected. He got down on his knees and, slowly, began picking up the torn pieces of work. One by one. Every fragment.

Though Manu was new, people respected him. He never played office politics or blamed others. He always stayed calm under pressure. That's why his quiet protest made such an impact.

He wasn't dramatic about it. Manu didn't make a speech or confront the bully. He just quietly collected the pieces like a puzzle, as if the work—and his dignity—were worth saving. Everyone watched. The director stood frozen, completely off guard. This wasn't the fight-or-flight reaction he expected.

Later, people weren't talking about the rejected campaigns or torn scripts. They talked about how one person reframed the conversation. Instead of dwelling on the past or blaming the bully, Manu chose to move forward.

"Manu didn't fight back," someone said. "He just didn't let the guy win."

Two weeks later, one of the senior creatives spoke up before the next review started. "We need some ground rules," he said to the director. "If you don't like the direction, give us guidance to continue exploring. But please don't tear up our work."

This story shows that courage isn't just for extraordinary people. Manu wasn't a rebel or a formal leader. He simply refused to surrender his voice. Sometimes the most powerful messages need no words—just the courage to address issues and move forward.

The Psychology of Courage

Here's what we often get wrong about courage: We think it's a personality trait we're either born with or without. The truth is far more encouraging.

Most of us are neither naturally courageous nor inherently cowardly. We make choices, moment by moment, whether to act or whether to wait for someone else to go first. The young creative who collected those torn scripts wasn't born brave. He simply chose to refuse surrender in that specific moment.

So, what separates those who act from those who don't?

Courage—derived from the French word *cœur* (heart)—means "to lead from the heart." It's not an impulsive *reaction* but a thoughtful *action* taken in pursuit of a worthwhile goal, despite significant perceived risk. Research by Matthew Howard on workplace courage shows it requires four elements:[52]

- **Willful choice:** deciding to act, not react
- **Worthwhile purpose:** serving others or defending principles
- **Perceived risk:** facing real stakes (social, professional, or personal)
- **Willingness to sacrifice:** accepting potential costs

This is what distinguishes courage from mere bravery, risk-taking, or confidence. At work, this means speaking up about problems, challenging flawed decisions, or defending colleagues, even when the outcome is uncertain.

Leaders often far overestimate how much organizational policy affects employee behavior. Yes, psychological safety impacts people's willingness to speak up. But personality matters just as much. Some people naturally question orders and challenge authority—they'll speak up regardless of the environment.

This doesn't mean that courage is fixed. You can develop traits like grit and a proactive personality through practice and choice. People act courageously when they decide to take ownership, regardless of conditions.

Most team members already have the capacity for acting with courage. But what they lack isn't fearlessness—they lack the belief that their acts can matter. Everything changes once you understand that courage is a skill you can strengthen, not something you're born with.

Acting with courage includes using your voice, having perspective, and taking responsibility. Your team needs a systematic approach for putting all three into practice.

CPR: Moving from Backward Talk to Forward Talk

When teams get trapped in blame, groupthink, or avoidance, they need more than good intentions to break free. They need systematic interventions to address what's been left unsaid or unresolved—the conversational debt.

The solution is **CPR—Courage, Perspective, and Responsibility**. These three interventions address the Pointlessness Paradox that I explained in Chapter 1, helping teams move away from Backward Talk patterns and into Forward Talk.

Just like medical CPR revives a failing heartbeat, conversational CPR restores the flow of healthy, productive dialogue to team interactions. When conversations flatline—when people stay quiet and teams avoid real issues, blame each other, or rush to false consensus—you need immediate intervention to restore healthy vitals.

The good news? Anyone can learn these conversation-saving techniques.

Here's what CPR looks like in action:

- **Courage:** The decision to speak up instead of surrendering your voice to silence. When you see something isn't being addressed, such as when people stay silent but look uneasy, you decide to name what needs attention.
- **Perspective:** The choice to share your views instead of surrendering your judgment to social pressure. You offer your reality, ideas, and questions, or challenge groupthink.
- **Responsibility:** The commitment to understanding what went wrong systemically instead of surrendering to the blame game. You examine what the team is responsible for and what you are responsible for, then own your part in the problem and the solution.

How CPR Drives Forward Talk

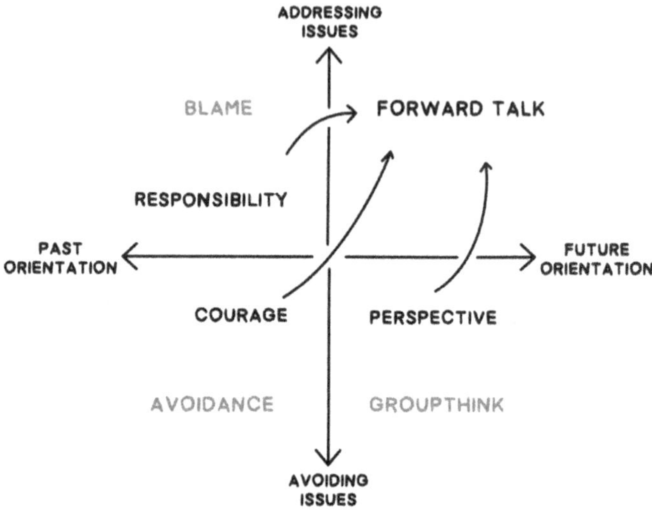

Manu, our young creative, demonstrated all three:

1. Courage to act when everyone else stayed silent.
2. Perspective that challenged the assumption that his work was worthless.
3. Responsibility for moving the situation forward instead of getting stuck in who was wrong.

Together, these are the building blocks of Forward Talk, and they're skills you can learn and practice.

From Avoidance to Forward Talk through Courage

When teams avoid critical topics—when important issues go unspoken, or when everyone can sense problems but conversations flatline—courage provides the intervention needed to get the dialogue flowing again.

The shift isn't about being a Hero (see more on that in Chapter 13). It's about recognizing that the conversations you avoid today become the crises you face tomorrow. Your voice becomes a tool for ensuring real issues get the attention they need:

- **In meetings:** "There's something we're not saying here that we need to address before we can move forward."
- **In team dynamics:** "I can sense tension here that's affecting our work. Let's address it before it gets worse."
- **In feedback:** "We're not pushing back hard enough on these design options. We need to raise our standards."

When you use your voice and speak up consistently, others learn that difficult conversations are survivable and valuable. Problems get smaller because your team catches them early.

From Groupthink to Forward Talk through Perspective

When teams rush to artificial consensus—when everyone nods too quickly, when dissent gets suppressed—your perspective restores the authentic pulse of diverse thinking that Forward Talk requires.

This means recognizing that your perspective has value even when it's unpopular or others disagree. Forward Talk requires cognitive diversity. Challenging assumptions strengthens decisions and helps teams address real concerns rather than overlooking them.

- **In strategic planning:** "What's our worst-case scenario if these assumptions are wrong? What aren't we seeing?"
- **In decision-making:** "Before we commit, what would our harshest critic say about this approach?"

- **In problem analysis:** "I sense there's disagreement in the room that we haven't surfaced. Who has concerns they haven't shared?"

Challenging assumptions turns you into an innovation catalyst. You show that being a good team player also includes addressing conflict openly. You choose professional honesty over comfortable consensus.

From Blame to Forward Talk through Responsibility

When teams get stuck analyzing past failures—focusing energy on finding fault instead of building solutions—taking responsibility shifts the conversation toward future-oriented action while addressing real issues.

This means developing genuine investment in team outcomes. Forward Talk requires people to take ownership of their part in the problem and the solution. Ownership is grounded in three drivers: **efficacy** (knowing your actions create results), **self-identity** (seeing team success as something meaningful), and **belonging** (feeling connected to teammates and shared purpose).

- **In decision-making:** "Let me start by sharing what I could have done better in my role, then let's figure out what needs to happen next."
- **In conflict resolution:** "I contributed to this tension by not sharing my objections sooner. Now let's solve it together."
- **In problem-solving:** "Here's how I can help fix this. I have resources and ideas that could make a difference."

Responsibility is contagious and turns you into a magnet for solutions. When you model it, your colleagues will stop protecting their reputation and start contributing. Problems stop being battles to win and start becoming puzzles to solve.

The Moments That Define You

Some moments seem ordinary but can change your life—even who you become. A split second when you sense something needs to be said. A meeting where you notice something is wrong, but everyone stays quiet. A conversation where you must choose between comfort and courage.

These moments feel small when they're happening. Insignificant, even. But in retrospect, they reveal and define who you are.

Remember Daniel Pink's research insight about regrets that I shared in Chapter 7? We don't regret the actions we took nearly as much as the actions we didn't take: The conversation we avoided. The time we chose to stay silent when a colleague was under attack. The bully we left unchallenged.

Life is full of these defining moments. They often arrive disguised as everyday choices, but they're decision points between two versions of yourself: The reluctant observer who waits for someone else to act, or the courageous participant who chooses to go first.

Think about your recent team interactions.

What signals have you been noticing?

Which ones did you fail to notice, or even ignore?

When you sensed something, did you hesitate?

What made you afraid?

Those moments are coming again—and when they do, you'll face the same choice that Manu did: Surrender your agency, or claim it.

Here's what these moments look like:

- **The forced alignment moment:** Your leader presents a new direction and immediately asks, "Are we all good with this?" Everyone nods, but you notice sideways glances and uncomfortable shifts. The energy feels off, like people are agreeing just to move on.

  You have a choice: Ignore the signs or make them visible.

- **The blame game moment:** A project has failed and your leader is attacking one department—and others are joining in without examining what actually went wrong. You can feel the heat. People care more about finding culprits than preventing similar problems.

  You have a choice: Join the finger-pointing, or break the pattern.

- **The missing voices moment:** You're in a room where the loudest personalities are making decisions that will primarily affect those who aren't speaking up. You can sense important perspectives being ignored.

  You have a choice: Let the extroverts dominate, or intentionally invite the quiet voices to share their concerns.

These moments compound into the person you become and the team culture you help create. When you give up, you're turning a defining moment into a surrender pattern. When you choose courage, you signal that speaking up matters.

Courage Spreads Faster Than You Think

Our actions create ripple effects we often don't see. When you model Forward Talk, you don't just do what's right for the team—you inspire others to do the same.

Harvard professor Dr. Jeff Polzer calls this the "vulnerability loop."[53] To create trust and belonging in a team, someone needs to send a vulnerability cue first. This might mean admitting a mistake, sharing that you're nervous, or asking for help. When one person takes this risk, others notice and reciprocate, creating a chain of honest behavior. Notably, the *second* person who responds is the most important link in this chain, continuing the behaviors you've introduced.

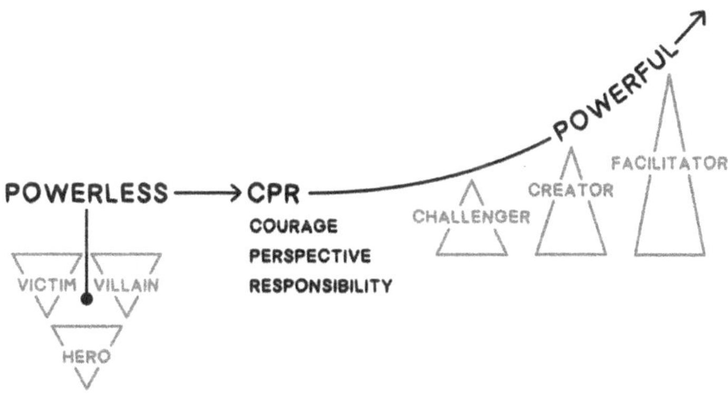

Something similar happens when you model Forward Talk:

1. Person A applies a CPR intervention—exhibits Courage to break through avoidance, shares their Perspective, or takes Responsibility.
2. Person B recognizes the shift into Forward Talk—they see that Backward Talk patterns can be changed.

3. Person B contributes their own CPR intervention, adding their Courage, Perspective, or Responsibility.
4. Person A feels supported.
5. A new team habit forms: Forward Talk becomes an expectation, not an exception.

Here's a real example of how this transformed a leadership team:

I was running a workshop for eight executives from an insurance company who'd been struggling for months. They were a team in name only. Their meetings felt like status updates where everyone focused on their own areas. I could feel the tension: Everyone was trying to protect their turf and judging others by their own standards.

Their self-assessment results showed they weren't operating at their full potential, lacked cohesion, and couldn't challenge each other openly.

"You're not really a team. You're just eight department heads who happen to meet in the same room," I challenged them directly. "When you refer to 'your' team, who do you think of? Hyla, I just heard you say 'my team' when talking about legal?"

The legal director looked surprised, then reciprocated honestly: "You're right. I think of my legal team first. I usually put their needs first in these discussions."

That bold admission opened the door for others. The CFO chimed in: "I see most everything through a finance lens. When something doesn't fit our processes, I get defensive. I know innovation needs to move quickly, but I tend to focus on financial risk first. We should discuss how to find a happy medium—how can we move faster without breaking important control policies?"

One by one, everyone joined in. They realized they were all viewing issues from their departmental perspectives rather than considering the whole company. When disagreements came up, everyone doubled down on what was good for their specific teams instead of the entire organization. This realization helped move the conversation forward.

We created team priorities using "even over" statements[54]—like "speed to market even over compliance perfection" and "strategic bets even over proven returns." Six weeks later, most executives were communicating more openly. They used these priorities as a measuring stick to make decisions based on what was good for the company overall, not just their areas. And all this happened because Hyla was willing to say what everyone was thinking. She responded to my challenge, reciprocated my signal, and started the loop.

Your three CPR interventions work the same way. When you own your part in a problem, colleagues start examining their own behaviors. When you challenge a popular idea, others feel more confident to voice their concerns. When you break the silence and address a difficult topic, people realize they're not alone.

If you're skeptical that these small ripples could create real change, thinking you must convince hundreds of people for Forward Talk to spread, the research tells a different story.

In his book *Change: How to Make Big Things Happen*, Professor Damon Centola suggests that a tipping point of just 25 percent can create a cascade effect across an entire organization.[55]

A McKinsey study found an even lower threshold—7 percent.[56] Organizations with just 7 percent of employees actively participating in culture transformation are twice as likely to deliver higher shareholder returns.

These early adopters are often called "fire-starters"—and for good reason. They ignite change.

You don't have to convert everyone—you just need to start a movement with the right people. In a team of twenty-one, you only need three. Choose strategically: someone with formal authority who turns conversations into action, someone with influence whom people naturally trust, and someone whose expertise gives their voice credibility.

It begins with you. Whenever you use your voice, own your part, or challenge groupthink, you encourage others to do the same and signal that being stuck is not an option. You invite others into a new kind of conversation built on collective courage.

Individual courage creates vulnerability loops. Vulnerability loops build collective courage. Collective courage transforms how your team operates.

Fire-starters[57] don't just light any fire—they choose when and where to spark them with purpose. You're not being difficult when you break Backward Talk patterns and model Forward Talk: You're liberating your team's thinking, freeing everyone from being stuck in the roundabout.

Stop waiting for perfect conditions. Start the fire.

From Backward Talk to Forward Talk

Backward Talk	Forward Talk
Stay silent because speaking up won't change anything	Speak up. Stop waiting for perfect conditions
The more you avoid issues, the more conversational debt piles up	Address issues while they're manageable
Get stuck circling the same conversations repeatedly	Recognize the three patterns trapping you: avoidance, blame, groupthink
Feel shut down by someone else's objections	Reframe conversational objections into possibilities
Surrender your voice to others' expectations	Reclaim your agency through CPR: Courage, Perspective, Responsibility
Adopt powerless roles: Victim, Villain, or Hero	Adopt powerful roles: Creator, Challenger, or Facilitator
Treat conversational problems as one-off issues	Build daily habits to prevent debt from accumulating

CHAPTER 15

A Forward Talk Culture

"Conversation takes time. We need time to sit together, to listen, to worry and to dream together."

—Margaret J. Wheatley

Remember the story from Chapter 2? At a presentation, a CEO attacked Zora for challenging his campaign choice, and I spoke up despite being new on the job. This taught me something crucial: Defining moments don't announce themselves.

I wasn't naturally the brave one. I was shy and young—usually the quiet one, expecting someone else would step in. But watching everyone stay silent while Zora was being put down, I realized something important: We all had the chance to make things right, but nobody was taking it.

That's what made me act—not fearlessness, but knowing that someone had to go first. Your voice only becomes powerful when you use it.

That defining moment became my template for how I show up—not reacting without thinking, but by being intentional. Not speaking up because I was fearless, but because I learned that courage isn't the absence of fear—it's about feeling fear but acting anyway.

When you feel that familiar tension—knowing you should speak up, but hesitating—you're standing at the edge of transformation. Sometimes fear protects us from real danger. Often, it just prevents us from taking the leap to becoming who we're meant to be.

Like any skill, Forward Talk isn't something you're born with. It develops through deliberate practice, support, and gradually taking on bigger challenges. This chapter shows you how to build that practice systematically.

Recognizing Your Defining Moments

You know the feeling. Your boss shares incorrect data, and you wonder: "Should I say something?" Everyone nods at an impossible timeline: "Do I go along, or challenge it?" A colleague takes credit for your work: "Do I let it go?"

These moments might seem small, but they're quietly shaping who you become. Learning to spot these moments is the first step in building Forward Talk. Here's how to become more aware:

Spot the Signals

Your body and surroundings give you clues about speaking-up opportunities before your mind realizes it. Like a smoke alarm, these signals indicate different levels of urgency—from mild awareness to urgent alerts.

Internal Signals

Signal	What You Might Feel
Hesitation (Low Risk)	Slight pause, minor shift in posture, brief break in eye contact, or a quiet "hmm." This is your body noticing something worth attention.
Doubt (Moderate Risk)	Faster heartbeat, stomach flutter, fidgeting, or leaning forward/back. Your body says, "Pay closer attention."
Urgency (High Risk)	Chest tightness, sweating, clenched jaw or fists, or gut reaction. Your body says, "Act now."
Danger (Crisis Point)	Racing pulse, fight-or-flight response, or strong urge to speak or leave. Something critical is at stake.

External Signals

Signal	What You Might See
The Silence That Speaks	When a room goes quiet after, "Any questions?" but you sense unasked concerns hanging in the air.
The Nervous Laughter	When people laugh awkwardly after sharing bad news or unrealistic timelines, showing discomfort they won't express.
The Eye Contact Avoidance	When colleagues look down, check their phones, or exchange glances instead of engaging with the discussion.
The Salesperson Smile	When a leader shows fake enthusiasm about a problematic decision, like they're trying to close a deal rather than solve an issue.
The Energy Drain	When meetings that should be energizing feel heavy, or people seem checked out despite nodding along.

For a couple of weeks, keep a "signal log." Each day, note three signals you noticed and when they happened (in a team meeting, during a one-on-one, etc.). Then reflect on any patterns and ask:

- Which signals do I notice most easily?

- What situations consistently trigger multiple signals?
- What happens if I don't act when I notice these signals?
- What signals does our team typically miss or ignore?
- How does our team usually respond when someone points out these signals?

Choose When to Act

Move from "I should probably say something" to "I will say something at this specific time." Don't wait for the perfect moment—create one. Schedule it: "Tomorrow's one-on-one with Alex" or "Friday's project update."

After identifying a defining moment, decide when to act and put it in your calendar. This removes the emotional hesitation and makes you more likely to follow through.

Getting Perspective

Conversational debt doesn't always take months to grow—sometimes small issues get worse within a day if not addressed. Problems that seem manageable today become much harder (and more expensive) to fix tomorrow.

Use the Twenty-Four-Hour Rule

When facing a defining moment, ask yourself:

- What will this issue look like if nobody addresses it this week?
- Who will be affected if this pattern continues for a month?
- What resources (time, money, or relationships) will fixing this later cost versus now?

- What opportunities are we missing while this remains unaddressed?

When you notice a defining moment, block off ten minutes to answer these questions. Write down what you discover. This helps you see the real cost of not acting.

Use the Regret Filter

Fast-forward six months. Will you regret speaking up, or will you regret staying silent?

The real question isn't whether the conversation feels risky now, but whether the long-term cost of silence outweighs the short-term discomfort of taking action.

Strategic Reflection Questions:

- Six months from now, will this issue have resolved itself or gotten worse?
- Am I avoiding this conversation to stay comfortable, at the cost of respect and trust later?
- What would I tell someone else to do in this exact situation?
- What conversations are we all avoiding that could quickly get worse?
- What opportunities for influence and relationship-building am I losing by staying silent?

This helps you assess real risks instead of just avoiding discomfort.

Building Support Networks

Some battles are too big to fight alone. When dealing with resistance to important changes or challenging long-standing patterns, joining forces with others will increase your odds of success.

Forward Talk Partners

Think of this like having a workout buddy, but for difficult conversations. Find colleagues who are also working on developing their skills, then create an accountability partnership. One team I know calls these "Truth Buddy" relationships. The key is mutual support, not one-way coaching.

Check in monthly about opportunities taken or missed. Share what you learned from tough conversations and get advice on tackling upcoming challenges. These conversations or check-ins might sound like:

- "I need to discuss an unrealistic timeline with my manager. How have you handled bringing up concerns to leadership?"
- "I spoke up in yesterday's meeting about the budget issues, and it went better than expected. Here's what worked when I framed the conversation in a constructive way."

Set specific commitments that feel challenging but doable: "We'll both speak up at least once in leadership meetings this month," or "We'll practice owning our part in the next project retrospective."

Having someone who understands the difficulty makes it easier to take social risks.

The best Forward Talk partnerships I've seen involve peers facing similar challenges, like two managers supporting each other's efforts to be more direct with senior leadership, or two team members helping each other navigate difficult peer relationships. Shared experiences create real understanding and practical advice.

Forward Talk Mentorship

If you're a leader, create formal mentoring relationships focused specifically on conversational skills. Pair newer team members with those who consistently demonstrate ownership and challenge groupthink.

Structure these relationships around skill transfer, not just general career advice. These mentoring conversations should focus on practical questions, such as:

- How do you prepare for difficult conversations?
- How do you frame challenges constructively?
- How do you recover when conversations go badly?
- How do you distinguish between productive confrontation and destructive criticism?

Regular mentoring sessions give teams a safe space to work through difficult situations and share strategies. One VP from one of my clients holds monthly "Forward Talk circles," where junior team members can bring challenging situations to discuss, and experienced colleagues can share how they've handled similar issues.

However, mentorship shouldn't just flow downward. Reverse mentoring is just as powerful. Junior employees often notice power dynamics and communication patterns that senior people miss, and can provide valuable insights into how leadership messages are received.

Build Strong Alliances

There's power in numbers: A leader might dismiss one person's concerns as resistance, but they can't ignore a united front.

I once worked with a senior team from a Canadian bank whose leader blocked a key initiative that everyone else wanted. Instead of each person fighting separately, I advised them to present their case together as one voice. They succeeded because a collective perspective carries more weight than individual pushback.

Build alliances before you need them. Find colleagues who share your values about quality, transparency, or customer focus. Build relationships so that when challenging moments arise, you can push back together.

Forward Talk Communities

Create informal learning groups within your organization where people practice better conversational skills together.

Meet monthly to share challenges, discuss difficult conversations, and practice approaches to common scenarios. Take turns facilitating so everyone has a chance to lead and contribute. Focus on actionable learning: Role-play upcoming difficult conversations, analyze what made past conversations effective, and share strategies that work in different contexts.

The best practice groups work like skill-sharing communities, where people bring real challenges they're facing, such as:

- "I need to tell my colleague that his interrupting hurts team dynamics. How can I frame that constructively?"
- "A client wants features that we know won't work, but saying no feels risky. How can we push back without sounding negative?"

These communities become spaces to intentionally practice Forward Talk with low risk. They also build a collection of best practices, storing wisdom about what works in your specific culture.

Team Foundations

Individual courage is powerful, but for lasting change, the whole team must share the responsibility. Your goal isn't to be the sole brave voice in the room, but to create conditions where Forward Talk becomes everyone's responsibility.

Team Conversational Agreements

The most effective teams write down explicit agreements about Forward Talk and hold one another accountable. Unlike generic team charters that nobody uses, these agreements focus specifically on how the team will handle difficult conversations and foster mutual support.

Work together to create specific commitments that address your team's challenges. For example:

- "We will raise concerns within forty-eight hours of noticing them."
- "We will ask, 'What's my part?' before blaming others."
- "We will challenge any decision that was made without customer input if it affects the customer."

The power isn't in the words but in the shared commitment. One marketing team agreed to "Avoid ending meetings with fake agreement—someone will always ask 'What are we not saying?'"

Another engineering team committed to "Challenge rushed technical decisions, even if it slows down the timeline."

Written agreements are just the start. For real change, teams must regularly check if they're following through, and be willing to call one another out when they're not.

Forward Talk Rituals

Team rituals are symbolic practices that connect members with shared purpose and values—they create meaning through repetition.[58] Unlike agreements (which codify specific behavioral norms), rituals help teams remember why difficult conversations matter in the first place.

Develop team practices that connect challenging conversations to shared values. A team ritual can remind people why speaking up matters, and what honest dialogue protects.

If you lead a team, create pre-meeting rituals that connect to your team's purpose:

- Start strategy meetings by asking, "What would we regret not discussing today?"
- Begin project retrospectives with, "How can we own our part in fixing systemic issues?"
- Open performance discussions with, "What kind of feedback would help each of us grow, even if it's hard to hear?"

These short prompts help teams focus on what matters most—customer needs, quality standards, team effectiveness, or organizational values. When difficult topics serve something bigger than personal comfort or reputation, speaking up feels purposeful rather than risky.

One engineering team I worked with developed a simple ritual called "Debug Now or Cry Later" for technical reviews. They spent two minutes identifying what was at stake: "If we don't challenge weak assumptions now, we'll be fixing bugs at 2 a.m. six months from now. If we don't surface integration concerns today, we'll be explaining to customers why their data is corrupted next quarter."

Grounding the conversation in tangible, real-world consequences made technical criticism feel protective rather than combative.

Forward Talk Recovery Protocols

Even with practice, Forward Talk can still go wrong. Someone challenges an idea and gets attacked. A team member voices an unpopular perspective and gets dismissed. People take social risks and face pushback instead of engagement.

Recovery protocols are immediate interventions that protect team members. Think of them as conversational first aid. Without recovery protocols, people learn that speaking up leads to negative consequences, and your Forward Talk culture dies.

When a conversation goes off track, here's how to respond in the moment—and afterward—to reinforce social courage:

- **In the moment:** When someone gets attacked for speaking up, redirect: "Let's focus on the concern itself, not whether it should have been raised." When someone shares an unpopular perspective, invite engagement: "Who else has thoughts on this point?"
- **Acknowledge the risk:** Recognize the courage to speak up. Say, "That took courage to share—let's make sure we really hear it," or "I appreciate you bringing up something

difficult." This reinforces that Forward Talk leads to engagement, not isolation.

- **After the meeting:** If someone's contribution was dismissed or they took a risk that didn't go well, check in privately: "How are you feeling about what happened in there?" Sometimes people need to process difficult conversations to stay willing to speak up in the future.

Recovery protocols won't eliminate all risks of speaking up, but they protect those who do take risks and reinforce a culture where Forward Talk is valued.

Your Forward Talk Culture Starts Now

You now have a complete framework for developing Forward Talk both personally and as a team. You can recognize Forward Talk moments by noticing physical and environmental signals. You understand how the Twenty-Four-Hour Rule and the Regret Filter can help you act before problems grow. You also know how and when to build alliances instead of tackling difficult conversations alone.

More importantly, you now have the blueprint for creating a Forward Talk culture. Through partnerships, mentorship, rituals, communities, agreements, and recovery protocols, you have the agency to make it everyone's responsibility to address real issues rather than relying on individual courage.

In the next chapter, we'll take this one step further: transforming the Backward Talk patterns of the Drama Triangle into productive and positive steps forward.

CHAPTER 16

From Drama to Ownership

"If you can't stand the heat, you'd better get out of the kitchen."

—Harry S. Truman

As we saw in Chapter 13, team members often fall into three roles that drain energy from conversations: Victim, Villain, or Hero. This Drama Triangle leads to Backward Talk patterns, so your team needs to be able to spot these roles and redirect that energy forward.

The CPR Canvas will help you identify these powerless roles and transform them into powerful ones. Instead of trying to get rid of the drama, you transform it into positive action.

Escape the Drama Triangle

The Drama Triangle is magnetic. When one person plays a role, others get pulled into matching roles. Each role connects to a specific Backward Talk pattern:

- **Victim → Avoidance:** "Nothing I say matters anyway, so why bother?" They surrender their voice to learned helplessness, waiting for someone else to act.
- **Villain → Blame:** "Someone needs to be held accountable for this mess." They surrender their power to cosmic justice, focusing energy on finding who's at fault instead of building solutions.
- **Hero → Groupthink:** "Let me solve this for everyone so we can all get along." They surrender their judgment to artificial harmony, avoiding disagreement and pushing for quick agreement.

The cycle is self-reinforcing, with each role feeding the others. Victims create drama, Villains attack, and Heroes try to control the conversation. And most often it's not just individuals, but the entire team that acts like Victims or Heroes.

Teams don't choose these roles on purpose. They get pulled in by familiar triggers:

- Pressure creates Victims: "We don't have time to handle this properly."
- Conflict creates Villains: "Someone messed up and needs to take the blame."
- A need for harmony creates Heroes: "Let me fix this so we can move on."

Most teams are so used to this dynamic that they think it's normal. They don't realize they're stuck in powerless patterns.

This exercise helps reframe those powerless roles. This is key to shift from Backward Talk patterns to Forward Talk approaches.

- **From Victim to Creator:** Instead of waiting to be rescued, Creators take charge of what they can control. They focus on outcomes rather than dwelling on obstacles.
- **From Villain to Challenger:** Instead of attacking others, Challengers raise issues constructively. They question things to improve decisions, not harm relationships.
- **From Hero to Facilitator:** Instead of fixing everyone's problems, Facilitators help others find solutions. They build team capacity rather than dependency.

As we discussed in Chapter 14, this transformation happens using the three CPR interventions: Courage (speaking up instead of staying silent), Perspective (sharing views instead of going along with the group), and Responsibility (addressing systemic issues instead of blaming others).

Use the CPR Canvas to Transform Your Team

CPR Canvas©

Reviving Team Conversations

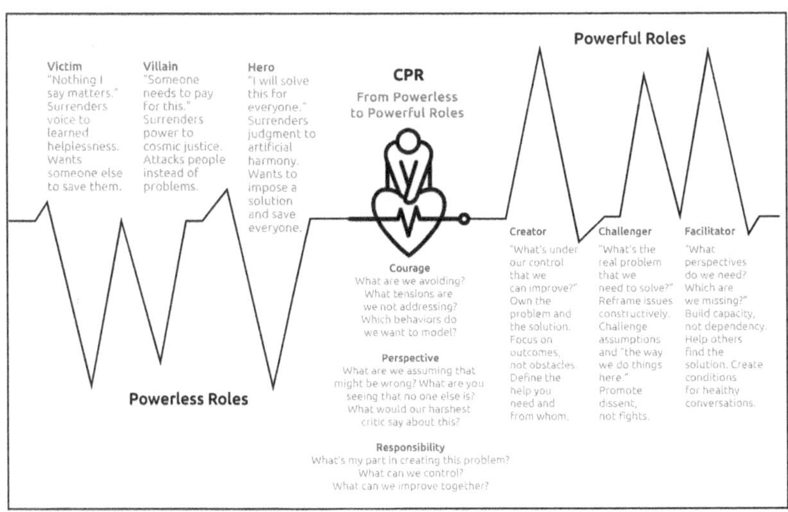

This canvas helps teams spot drama dynamics and redirect that energy toward powerful alternatives. Here's how to facilitate it:

Step 1: Set the Stage

Introduce the Drama Triangle and its roles. Make it clear that everyone falls into these roles eventually. The goal here isn't to judge anyone, but to recognize team patterns—the first step to regaining agency.

Step 2: Personal and Team Reflection

Start with silent individual reflection. Ask each person to consider:

- Which powerless role do I usually play when I'm under pressure?
- When do I act like a Victim, Villain, or Hero? Why?

No sharing yet—this is just for self-awareness.

Then look at team patterns and ask aloud, "As a team, which role do we usually fall into under pressure?"

Map recent stuck conversations:

- **Team Victim:** "The leadership team never listens to our recommendations."
- **Team Villain:** "Sales always overpromises and expects us to deliver miracles."
- **Team Hero:** "Let's solve this ourselves since the other teams don't get it."

Step 3: Apply CPR Intervention

Reflect on the following questions as a team:

Issues of Courage:

- What are we avoiding?
- What tensions are we not addressing?
- Which behaviors do we want to model?

Issues of Perspective:

- What are we assuming that might be wrong?
- What are you seeing that no one else is?
- What would our harshest critic say about this?

Issues of Responsibility:

- What's my part in creating this problem?
- What can we control?
- What can we improve together?

Step 4: Define Powerful Roles

Use your CPR insights to reframe roles from powerless to powerful. Remember to focus on the future rather than getting stuck in past issues.

Creator: "What's under our control that we can improve?"

- Own the problem and the solution
- Focus on outcomes, not obstacles
- Define the help you need and from whom

Challenger: "What's the real problem that we need to solve?"

- Reframe issues constructively
- Challenge assumptions and "the way we do things here"
- Promote dissent, not fights

Facilitator: "What perspectives do we need? Which are we missing?"

- Build capacity, not dependency
- Help others find the solution
- Create conditions for healthy conversations

Take Back Your Power

The CPR Canvas helps your team turn drama into ownership. When you notice Victim thinking, you redirect it to Creator behaviors that focus on control and outcomes. When you spot Villain patterns, you can channel that energy into constructive Challenging. When you see Hero behaviors, encourage the team to Facilitate conversations rather than being the rescuer.

Your team will gain three main benefits: conversations that address real issues instead of dancing around symptoms, better decisions because diverse perspectives have been considered, and conflicts that strengthen rather than damage relationships.

Your team already has the power needed for better conversations. The CPR Canvas shows you how to take it back.

PART III RECAP

Reclaim Your Voice

In Summary:

Most teams surrender their voice without realizing it. This doesn't happen because people lack opinions but because they fall into unhealthy patterns. Some default to blame (surrendering their power to cosmic justice), choose avoidance (surrendering their voice to silence), or fall into groupthink (surrendering their judgment to social pressure).

The Drama Triangle shows three powerless roles people play: Victim, Villain, and Hero.

The solution is CPR. Have the Courage to share your Perspective and take Responsibility for your part.

Key Takeaways:

- Defining moments don't announce themselves. Every day, you can choose to claim your power instead of giving it away.
- Courage spreads through loops: Speak up first and find someone who reciprocates. Others will follow.
- Reframe powerless roles into powerful ones: from Victim to Creator, Villain to Challenger, and Hero to Facilitator.
- "Fire-starters" know things get better after you act, not before. Go start the fire.

From Conversational Debt to Forward Talk

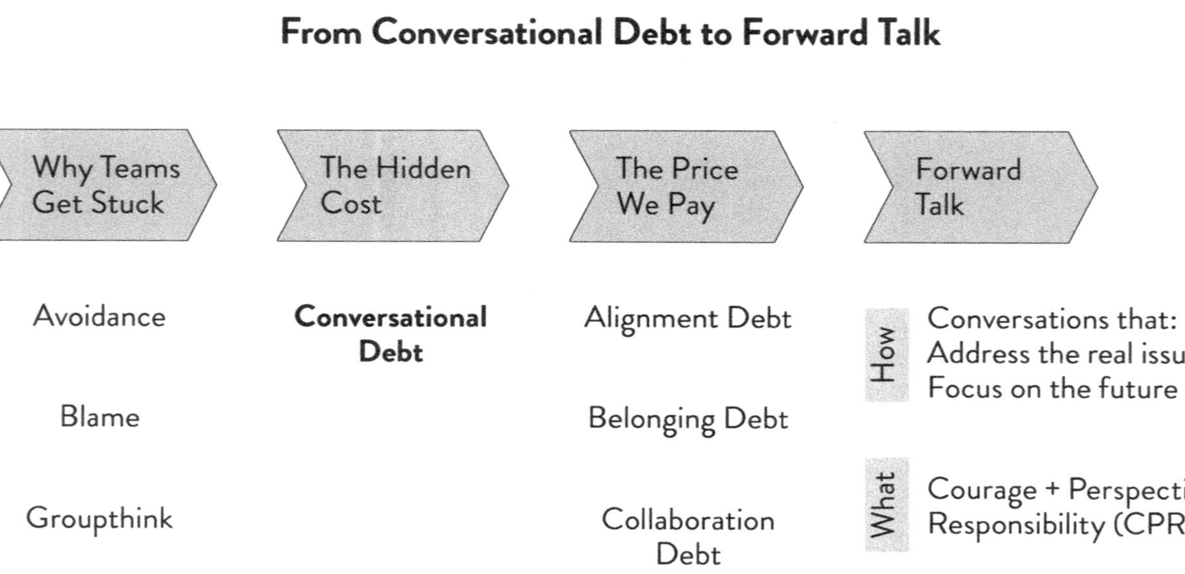

Before You Finish

You now know how to spot what's stopping your team from having better conversations—and how to fix it.

Ready to use Forward Talk with your team? Start here:

- Take the quiz to identify your team's conversational debt
- Use the templates to surface difficult topics
- Check the resources to choose where to start

Go to gustavorazzetti.com/forward-talk-tools
or scan the QR code below.

PART IV

Move Forward

CHAPTER 17

Forward Talk in Action

"The real voyage of discovery consists not in seeking new landscapes, but in having new eyes."

—Marcel Proust

By now, you have a better understanding of why teams get stuck (Part I), how conversational debt accumulates (Part II), and how Forward Talk helps you reclaim your agency (Part III). Now it's time to move from insight to action.

At this point, you might be thinking: *Great, now I need to completely retrain my team and replace all these ingrained Backward Talk patterns with new ones.*

Not necessarily. I'm going to show you a different approach: reframing.

Just like judo uses an opponent's force against them, reframing leverages the strength of Backward Talk patterns to redirect them into Forward Talk. Instead of trying to ignore or erase negative patterns, you'll learn to channel them in your favor. The power isn't in fighting these patterns, but in redirecting them.

Let me show you how this works in practice, starting with a moment that changed everything.

Giving Conversations a Last Chance

I was once hired as the last resort. Literally. I usually get called in late in the game—when Backward Talk patterns are already the norm, but the team still has some hope. Yet this time felt different. The first call with the HR executive didn't sit right, and I sensed there was something bigger going on than simply their needing help integrating an acquired company.

When I spoke with Andrew, the company COO, my suspicions were confirmed. This multibillion-dollar tech company had gone through multiple acquisitions, but none like this. They'd acquired a tech platform in the healthcare space—a new area for them—and everything was moving in the wrong direction: the culture, the integration, the business, and the efficiencies. He was blunt: I was his last resort. Either we would find a path forward, or they would have to undo the deal.

What happened next wasn't a miracle or the result of some special superpower. I simply helped them reframe their existing conversations.

After all, Forward Talk isn't just about having the right process or using the right tools. It's a system built around courage, and courage sometimes has to start with us as facilitators of conversations. To succeed, I had to model the courage I was asking them to find.

When There's Nothing Left to Lose

After interviewing team members from both sides, the pattern was clear: Everyone believed both companies were better off before the acquisition, and both sides regretted the deal. Teams were stuck in the past, blaming each other.

My initial impulse was to tell the client there was no hope, particularly when people demonstrated no interest in turning things around.

After consulting with my team, we decided to give it a try anyway. We were the last resort, and I'm not one to give up easily. However, I also knew that a standard approach wouldn't work. I had to set a completely different tone before we even met with the client.

I asked participants to complete an unconventional pre-work exercise: write their own obituary. I use this exercise sparingly, mostly when I need to break through deep resistance. This isn't about career accomplishments—it's about confronting our own mortality and reflecting on how we want to be remembered, the legacy we want to leave behind.

It's a very powerful exercise, but it's also dangerous. Most people don't want to think about their own death, and even fewer want to discuss it with work colleagues. As a facilitator, you need the confidence to ask people to go there as well as the skills to hold space for deeply personal conversations.

The tension was palpable the moment we gathered. We started slowly, warming up the room before I asked everyone to share their obituaries. Many hesitated, but eventually everyone spoke up. A few cried, and two participants even left the room briefly. But something remarkable happens in this exercise: When you confront your own mortality, petty rivalries suddenly feel absurd.

This conversation created deep humanity without me having to ask them to be vulnerable. They stopped seeing one another as enemies, and started seeing other human beings with the same dreams, struggles, weaknesses, and hopes as themselves.

Surfacing What Everyone Was Thinking

With their defenses down, the next deliberate step I took was using the Stinky Fish method to surface tensions. This tool, which I'll explain in more detail in Chapter 18, serves as a metaphor for unresolved issues that eventually start to rot and stink. We asked participants to share their anxieties about the deal and their jobs—to voice what everyone was thinking but no one was saying.

Of course, we still faced some resistance. Many were reluctant to continue exploring. But my response to that resistance was timely, especially considering the obituary reflection: "What's the worst that can happen? That the deal will be undone? Well, so be it. If that's what everyone wants, your honesty will only accelerate the process."

Changing the tone requires more than a one-off activity. We debriefed the Stinky Fish in groups of two, where teams from each "side" shared their issues with each other, then with other subgroups. Finally, each side presented its common themes to the entire group. As expected, both sides claimed they were better off before and blamed the other party for all the problems.

Here's the crucial part: We didn't get into a debate. Rather than arguing over who was right or who caused which problem, we focused on building everyone's courage muscle. People began to feel more comfortable (and relieved) after sharing their feelings openly with the group. Writing things down has a remarkable effect: It helps people gain clarity by removing the emotional fog and confusion that surround the issues we ruminate on.

Arguments became grounded in facts rather than emotions. Though some blame persisted, it was now supported with evidence. People began addressing the real issues, meaning they were finally having the same conversations with the other side that they'd previously had in private with just their own teams.

Reframing from Past to Future

The next reframe was crucial. Instead of dwelling on what they'd lost (control, freedom, simplicity, and identity), I asked them to identify what had actually *improved* because of the acquisition. This wasn't wishful, positive thinking—it was forcing them to see the benefits they'd been blind to while they were grieving what was gone.

That shift was immediate. Suddenly, they could see tangible improvements that had been previously invisible when they were focused on loss.

This simple exercise helped the team shift from Backward Talk—"This acquisition was a mistake"—to Forward Talk: "What capabilities do we have now that we didn't have before?" This reframe transformed their perspective from past-focused blame to future-focused possibility.

Then came the third reframe. We moved to the Culture Evolution Canvas, a tool I use to integrate the cultures of two organizations. It addresses four key areas:

1. What we need to eliminate (things that no longer serve the team or never did).
2. What we need to accept (things that are out of our control).
3. What we need to preserve (good mindsets, practices, and behaviors from both sides).
4. What we need to create (what the new organization needs that both sides can help build).

This reframed the conversation entirely toward the future: building something together. It was about bringing together the best of each side while letting go of the past and what was beyond their control. The energy and body language in the room changed completely. They were no longer Victims, Villains, or Heroes, but Creators regaining control of their future. They began to realize that although someone once had the foresight to bring these two organizations together, what they'd missed were the effective conversations about how to do just that.

Leaders had rushed to sell the long-term benefits of the deal, but executives and team members had never been given a space for honest discussions about the hard parts of integration—the bad and the ugly, not just the good. That's how the conversational debt quickly piled up.

The Power of Reframing Conversations

What transformed this situation wasn't magic. It came from systematic reframing.

Reframing helps teams see their situation differently without changing the facts. You don't ask people to ignore their concerns or to completely change. Instead, you redirect their existing energy toward solutions. The problems stay real, but the possibilities for addressing them expand dramatically.

This approach is effective because it works with human psychology, not against it. Instead of making people defensive, you offer a new way to interpret the same facts. This helps people step back from their frustrations while still feeling heard.

When teams get stuck in Backward Talk patterns, they're trying to protect themselves from blame, losing control, uncertainty, and conflict. Instead of trying to eliminate these fears, reframing turns that energy into action.

The benefits are immediate and enduring. Teams move from defensive to curious, from stuck to capable, from feeling like Victims to becoming Creators of their future. Most importantly, they own the change. You're not imposing new patterns, but helping them use their existing energy more productively.

This approach works in three ways:

1. **Reframing in the moment** means catching Backward Talk patterns as they happen and redirecting them right away (as we explored in Chapter 5).
2. **Strategic reframing** means designing processes and systems that make Forward Talk easier.
3. **Prevention reframing** helps teams avoid relapsing into Backward Talk patterns after making progress.

The tools you'll explore aren't rigid templates to follow—they're ways to reframe conversations. Each requires different skills and serves different purposes, but they all share the same principle: Meet teams where they are, honor their energy, and redirect that energy forward.

The next chapters show you how to make this happen. You'll get tools and exercises to spot Backward Talk patterns and turn them into progress:

- **Chapter 18: Forward Talk Practices** shows you how to build Forward Talk muscle. These systematic approaches address root causes, not just symptoms.
- **Chapter 19: Preventing Future Debt** helps you keep your team from sliding back into unproductive loops.
- **Chapter 20: The Forward Talk Canvas** brings everything together, helping you plan your path forward and choose the right solutions for your team.

Let's do this.

CHAPTER 18

Forward Talk Practices

Chapter 5 showed you how to reframe conversations in the moment, catching Backward Talk patterns as they emerge to redirect them in real time. Now we're going system-wide: strategic reframes that address the root causes of Backward Talk patterns.

These solutions work at the source. Instead of managing the symptoms—simply working through conversations one by one—you'll transform the underlying conditions that make blame feel satisfying, avoidance feel safe, and groupthink feel harmonious.

You'll find two types of solutions: **Reframing Mindsets** (which change how teams think about conversations) and **Forward Talk Tools** (which are structured exercises you can facilitate with your team).

Pick the approach that tackles your team's most persistent issues. You don't need to use all these solutions—just those that address your biggest conversational debt.

Reframing Mindsets

These exercises will help reframe how your team thinks about conversations. From recovering agency to taking perspective, they will help address difficult conversations in a more productive and efficient way. The purpose of these exercises is not to fix all conversations, but to dismantle the limiting mindsets that get in the way of having them.

Recovering Team Agency

Backward Talk Pattern It Addresses: Avoidance

Goal: Shift from "nothing will change" to taking ownership

When teams avoid difficult conversations, they often develop learned helplessness about specific situations. They believe speaking up won't change anything, so they stop trying. This creates a vicious cycle where silence breeds more silence, and teams become convinced that authentic dialogue is impossible in their context.

This exercise will help your team break avoidance patterns by learning from their own positive experiences. Instead of focusing on why conversations don't work, teams identify when they did work, then try to recreate those conditions.

How It Works:

Most teams fall into the trap of believing that problems are personal (our fault), permanent (won't change), and pervasive (affect everything). Teams develop these explanations about their communication: "We're just bad at difficult conversations," "These conversations never work for us," or "We can't handle conflict."

This exercise challenges these explanations by reframing them:

- **From internal to external:** Instead of "We're bad at this" (internal), reframe to "We were under stress, which didn't help the conversation" (external).
- **From permanent to temporary:** Instead of "Addressing tensions in the open never works" (permanent), reframe to "That particular conversation didn't go as planned" (temporary).
- **From general to specific:** Instead of "We are bad at giving feedback" (general), reframe to "We struggle with addressing individual performance issues" (specific).

How to Apply It:

Start by naming your team's particular avoidance patterns. Instead of vague statements like "We avoid conflict," identify concrete situations: "Our post-mortems always turn into blame sessions" or "Strategy meetings feel like everyone just agrees because we're tired of endless debates."

Next, examine why you avoid these conversations. What typically goes wrong? Who usually gets defensive? What outcomes do you anticipate that make it feel safer not to engage at all? This builds awareness of the learned helplessness pattern.

Then, find your success stories. Think of times when difficult conversations actually worked well for your team. What's an example of when someone spoke up and sparked positive change? What difficult topic did you address that improved team dynamics? Every team has these moments, even if they don't realize it, or if it takes a while to remember them.

Finally, analyze what made those successes possible. What was different about the timing, setting, or approach? Who was involved, and how did they contribute? Use these insights to approach current avoided conversations by recreating the conditions that enabled your past successes. This will help your team regain the agency—and confidence—to handle difficult conversations. They just need to recreate the conditions that worked well in the past.

The Three Perspectives

Backward Talk Pattern It Addresses: Groupthink
Goal: Shift from "rushing to support an idea" to challenging assumptions

Most teams rely on individual courage to challenge ideas, which means dissent depends on personality traits rather than on a systematic approach. When questioning assumptions becomes everyone's job, teams make better decisions.

This exercise makes it more effective to review or challenge ideas by intentionally designing three different points of view.

How It Works:

Traditional devil's advocate approaches often fall short because they feel artificial or make someone the permanent "difficult person." Instead, this exercise invites three different perspectives: the Champions, the Explorers, and the Skeptics. Each analyzes the idea from different, integrated angles rather than choosing one over the other. The sum of all the points of view helps the team make better, more informed decisions.

How to Apply It:

When facing a complex decision, divide your team into three groups to analyze the proposal from different perspectives.

The Champions: Your job is to build the strongest case for the proposed decision—to define the best that can happen. Gather supporting evidence, address potential objections, and demonstrate why this approach will work.

The Explorers: Your job is to map the terrain honestly. What alternatives haven't we considered? What would a completely different approach look like? Your goal isn't to prove the idea wrong—it's to expand possibilities.

The Skeptics: Your job is to stress-test assumptions and uncover the worst that can happen. What are we taking for granted? Where might this approach fail? What questions haven't we asked yet? Your goal is not to blanketly reject solutions, but to highlight what others are missing.

After each team member presents their perspective, rotate roles so everyone can argue from a different position.

Debrief with these questions:

- Which role felt the most natural for each team member?
- What did we discover when forced to explore instead of champion?
- When we switched perspectives, what surprised us most?
- When making decisions, do we typically behave more like Champions, Explorers, or Skeptics?

Integrate all three perspectives to make your final decision. Role rotation prevents anyone from becoming the permanent pessimist while ensuring decisions get examined from multiple points of view. Teams will also discover that their colleagues are neither inherently negative nor positive—each perspective adds value.

Rapid Recovery from Mistakes

Backward Talk Pattern It Addresses: Blame
Goal: Shift from "sweeping mistakes under the rug" to learning and recovering from them

When teams fear mistakes, they waste energy hiding problems and pointing fingers instead of bouncing back. This exercise helps teams distinguish between different types of mistakes, as well as focus on rapid recovery and applied learning rather than blame and cover-ups.

How It Works:
Teams that master rapid recovery turn setbacks into competitive advantages. However, most organizations have a weird relationship with mistakes—some can't tolerate them, while others celebrate mistakes despite missing the point entirely. First, not all mistakes are equal: Some are goldmines of learning opportunities, yet others are sloppy oversights. Also, celebrating mistakes—and even learning from them—is not enough. Successful teams need to recover from the mistakes, from quickly fixing the consequences to applying what they've learned.

This exercise is about helping your team learn how to recover from mistakes quickly, not just to celebrate them.

How to Apply It:

Start by discussing the four types of mistakes with your team:

Sloppy Mistakes: These are daily errors that are easily preventable—sending emails without proofreading them, joining meetings with mics turned off, or arriving late. These need process fixes and accountability, not lengthy analysis.

Beginner Mistakes: These are the inevitable errors that happen when learning new skills or roles. These include both "a-ha moments" (unintended learning from ignorance) and "learning moments" (intentional practice leading to progress). Every beginner mistake should lead to measurable improvement.

Avoidance Mistakes: These are the result of trying to prevent errors by avoiding risks entirely—being unwilling to try a new process or hesitant to incorporate a workflow change. Teams spend enormous energy playing it safe, missing opportunities to discover or learn.

Goldmine Mistakes: From intentional trial-and-error experiments to trying new approaches, these "portals of discovery" can provide valuable insights. Take, for example, Unilever testing forty-five generations of detergent nozzles to find the perfect solution.

Next time your team makes a mistake, have them go through these conversational frameworks:

- **The Recovery Conversation (immediately):** When mistakes happen, gather the team and ask three forward-focused questions: "What can we do right now to minimize impact?" "What's our immediate next step?" "Who needs to know, and what do they need to know?" Skip "Whose fault was this?" entirely—there's time for analysis later.

- **The Learning Debrief (within a week):** Hold a structured conversation using this framework: "What specifically went wrong?" "How could we have prevented this?" "What will we do differently next time?" "What systems or processes need to change?" Document the answers and assign who will do what and by when.
- **The Pattern Check (monthly):** Review previous debrief agreements and ask: "Which changes from our recent debriefs have we actually implemented?" "What's preventing us from following through on the lessons we learned?" Focus on turning insights into actions rather than just collecting more insights.

Create team agreements about handling each type of mistake—what conversations you'll have, who will get involved, and how quickly you'll bounce back.

The Conversational Observer

Backward Talk Pattern It Addresses: All patterns (blame, groupthink, and avoidance)
Goal: Shift from "acting on autopilot" to noticing conversational patterns

Teams often operate unconsciously, repeating the same conversational patterns without realizing what gets in the way. This approach builds the internal capacity for recognizing and adjusting team behavior without needing external tools or help. It develops the ability to surface both positive and negative patterns, which can be maintained, improved, or eliminated.

How It Works:

Most teams operate in a state of unconscious competence: They've developed communication habits that feel automatic but aren't necessarily effective. The Conversational Observer role creates "meta-cognitive awareness"—the ability to think about thinking. When someone steps outside the conversation to watch the process, they spot patterns that participants miss while engaged in discussion.

This approach works because awareness is the first step in choice. Teams can't interrupt patterns they don't see, but once behaviors become visible, they become changeable.

How to Apply It:

During your next team meeting, assign one person to be the Conversational Observer. Have them monitor team dynamics using these lenses:

- **Speaking Patterns:** Which voices consistently dominate, and which are missing? Where or when are people seeking approval? Which topics does the team tend to soften or avoid to keep the peace?
- **Dealing with Ideas:** What happens when someone shares a half-formed thought? Does the team explore risky ideas or resort to safe ones? How are minority opinions treated? Do team members shut down ideas, impose their own, or build off one another's thoughts while adopting a "yes, and . . . " approach?

- **Energy Shifts:** What topics or moments seem to energize the room? Which ones drain the energy? When do people lean in versus check out? What behaviors inflate or deflate the team?
- **Managing Ambiguity:** What happens when no one has the answer? How do team members navigate uncertainty? Do they rush to premature solutions or sit comfortably with not knowing? How do team members communicate when there is not a clear answer yet?
- **Handling Conflict:** What happens when two perspectives collide? How does the team manage disagreements? Do team members suppress tension, or channel it productively? Is conflict addressed in the meeting or afterward?

After the meeting, spend five minutes debriefing on what the Conversational Observer noticed. Focus on patterns rather than individual behaviors. Rotate the observer role so everyone gets to see the team's culture from the outside.

Delivering Bad News

Backward Talk Pattern It Addresses: Blame

Goal: Shift from "messengers get shot" to rewarding those who deliver bad news

Let's face it—nobody likes delivering bad news. It's uncomfortable, risky, and sometimes feels like stepping into a storm you didn't create. But avoiding it? That only makes the storm worse.

How It Works:

Think about weather reporters. They deliver terrible forecasts all the time—hurricanes, blizzards, and heat waves—but we don't blame them for causing the weather. We need them to tell us what's coming so we can prepare.

The same principle applies at work. Teams need accurate information, even when it's not what anyone wants to hear. Unfortunately, team members often deliver bad news as if they were causing the problem. They apologize excessively, try to soften the blow, or dance around the issue, making people worry about what they're about to reveal.

This exercise will help your team deliver bad news like weather reporters do—factually, timely, and with clear implications. The team should focus on how to adapt to the bad weather forecast rather than shoot the messenger.

How to Apply It:

- **Get to the Point—and Use Facts:** Getting to the point quickly prevents anxiety from piling up. Support your message with specific, up-to-date information to keep the focus on facts rather than feelings. Instead of saying, "Our clients are unhappy," say, "Our customer satisfaction scores have declined by 20 percent this quarter."
- **Focus on What Needs to Happen:** Share the issue concisely, then steer the conversation toward what needs to happen. Instead of saying, "We're behind schedule," try, "Now that we're behind schedule, where would our resources be best allocated to meet critical milestones?" Frame it as a shared challenge.

- **Choose the Right Timing:** Plan your communication for a moment when your team is likely to be more receptive. Avoid catching leaders off guard, or delivering bad news during high-stress periods. When in doubt, ask to schedule time to discuss something important.
- **Present Initial Options:** Present a few starting points—alternative solutions, quick fixes, or thought-provoking questions—to kick off the conversation. Use the "What? (Event) So what? (Implications) Now what? (Potential scenarios)" framework to structure your message.
- **Acknowledge the Emotional Response:** Show empathy by acknowledging people's emotions, especially those who are deeply involved in the project. Saying something like, "I know how important this project is to you" demonstrates respect for their work and reduces defensiveness.
- **Own Your Part:** Take responsibility for any role you or your team may have had in the situation. This doesn't mean over-apologizing—it's about taking ownership. For instance, "We've had some setbacks that have impacted our progress, and here's what we're doing to get back on track."
- **Engage with Open-Ended Questions:** Use powerful questions like these to invite problem-solving: "What's your perspective on how we should approach this?" or "Where do you think we should focus next?" This turns delivering bad news into a future-oriented conversation.

Forward Talk Tools

These tools provide facilitated exercises for immediate implementation. Unlike conceptual approaches that can be adopted gradually, these require dedicated time blocks and clear process facilitation. Each addresses a specific debt type through systematic intervention.

The Stinky Fish

Backward Talk Pattern It Addresses: Avoidance

Goal: Surface issues and tackle conversational debt

Teams often avoid conversations about issues everyone can sense but no one wants to name directly. The "stinky fish"[59] represents those unspoken concerns that everyone can smell but no one dares acknowledge—the performance problem everyone sees, the strategy that feels wrong, or the relationship tension affecting the whole team. The longer we avoid cleaning up these rotting fish, the stinkier they get.

This exercise creates a structured way to surface what everyone is thinking but no one is saying. Using metaphor and progressive sharing, it makes dangerous topics safe to discuss, and it transforms individual concerns into collective issues worth addressing. Most importantly, it moves the conversation from sharing to problem-solving, reinforcing the idea that speaking up is worth the risk.

How It Works:

The process builds courage progressively by prompting reflection in small groups first. Starting in pairs reduces the risk of being the lone voice raised, while the requirement to narrow down issues at each stage forces teams to prioritize what matters most. Basically, if an issue doesn't make it to the next round, it won't get addressed.

How to Apply It:

This exercise has two steps, using one canvas each.

Canvas 1: Uncover the Stinky Fish

Individual Reflection: Each person privately identifies their stinky fish across four quadrants:

- What are your uncertainties?
- What's making you feel afraid or anxious?
- What is everybody thinking, but no one is saying?
- What are the past issues we can't get over?

Have everyone write these down without sharing, creating courage through anonymity.

Paired Sharing: Next, it's time to discuss. Have team members partner up and share their list of stinky fish. Both partners must agree on *three* issues (across all quadrants) to present. Challenge them: The issues that don't make it to the next round won't be addressed. This forces people to address real stinky fish problems, not superficial ones.

Groups of Four: Two pairs merge and share their three stinky fish each. The group of four must agree on which three issues should be moved to the next round.

Teams of Eight: Two groups of four merge, share their three issues each, and agree on the final three that are shared with the larger group.

Uncover the Stinky Fish©

Speaking up is the first step to solve silent problems

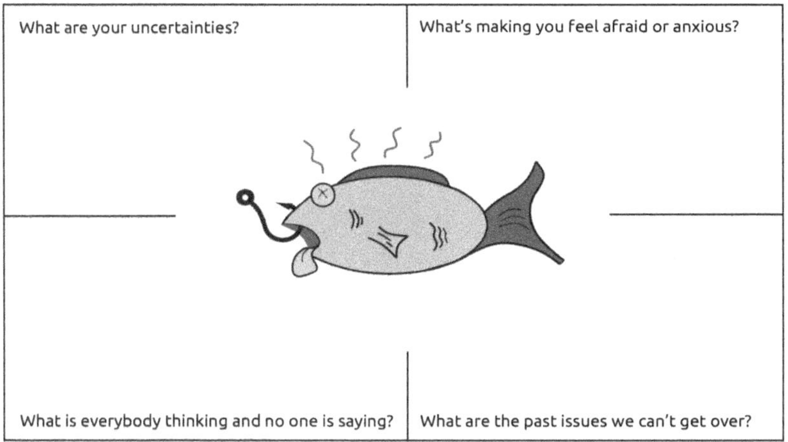

Canvas 2: Address the Stinky Fish

Consolidate: Capture the top three stinky fish from each team of eight, organized by quadrant (uncertainties, anxieties, what everyone's thinking, or past issues).

Categorize: Sort all issues into Quick Wins (small, simple changes that can build momentum) or Big Wins (longer-term structural changes requiring more effort and time).

Select and Plan: Choose three total issues to address: two Quick Wins and one Big Win. For each selected issue, brainstorm solutions and agree on who will lead the implementation and by when.

The progressive narrowing ensures only the most important issues get addressed, while the expanding group sizes prove that these problems are often shared concerns merely waiting for someone to break the silence. Most importantly, it proves that naming the stinky fish doesn't kill the messenger—it's actually the first step to cleaning up the problem.

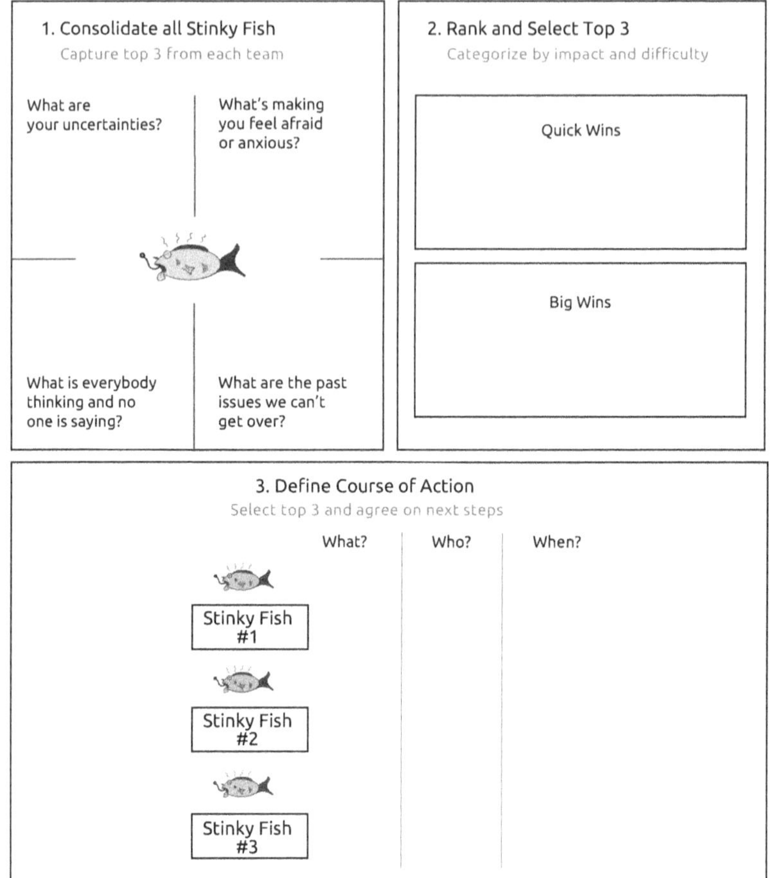

Cultural Tensions Canvas

Backward Talk Pattern It Addresses: Groupthink

Goal: Shift from "avoiding tensions" to using tensions as building blocks

The word "tension" has a bad rap in the workplace for all the wrong reasons. We've been taught that successful teams should be harmonious and always aligned. However, that's far from the truth.

Even the most successful teams face tensions. While often viewed as negative side effects, tensions are actually vital signs of a living, breathing organization. Like suspension bridges that can absorb heavy stresses between opposing forces, such as wind or heavy traffic, successful teams embrace tensions effectively.

This tool is ideal when external events disrupt a team—a new manager joins, a client is lost, a project goes wrong, or a valued member leaves. These disruptions trigger emotions, shape mindsets, and change behaviors. Instead of avoiding or trying to eliminate these tensions, teams must understand and channel them productively.

How It Works:

Teams often see tension as something to eliminate rather than leverage. However, tension between opposing forces—like ambition vs. sustainability, or innovation vs. quality—actually holds organizations together. When teams can integrate these tensions, they can reframe limiting patterns into liberating ones.

Emotions, mindsets, and behaviors can be both positive and negative depending on their impact. Frustration about budget cuts can fuel motivation to succeed despite constraints. Anxiety about a new leader can transform into curiosity about their leadership style and what will improve or stay the same.

Cultural Tensions Canvas©

Tensions can hold teams together, or tear them apart

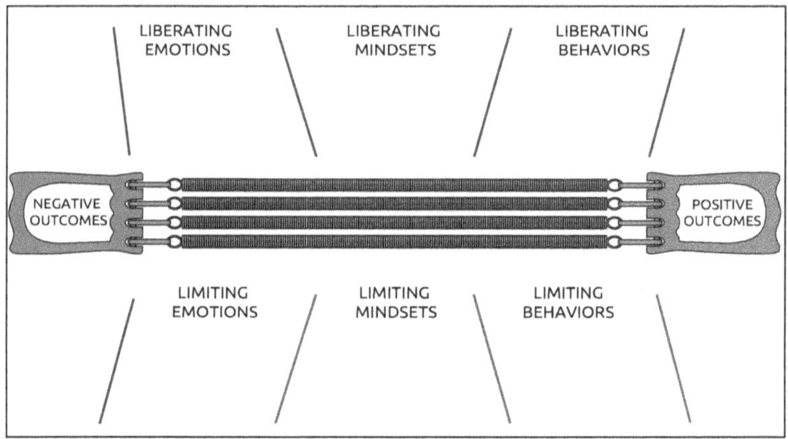

How to Apply It:

First, clarify the terms. *Emotions* are how we feel. *Mindsets* are the beliefs and thoughts that filter how we see our current and future state. *Behaviors* are what we do—our actions, ways of doing things, and rituals.

Next, allow the team to list examples of these on the canvas, posting it on a whiteboard or printed template. Give participants time to capture their ideas on sticky notes, one section at a time, in any order they want, and add them to the canvas. Consider the following questions for each section:

Limiting Emotions: Individual and collective feelings that frustrate the team and hinder performance

- How does the team feel about this recent event/change?
- What emotions drain our energy?
- Which feelings make us want to avoid discussing the issue?
- What emotions often surface when we face setbacks?

Liberating Emotions: Individual and collective feelings that produce excitement and move the team forward

- How does the team feel when performing at its best?
- What emotions energize us to tackle challenges?
- Which feelings make us want to collaborate more?
- What emotions help us bounce back from failure/bad news?

Limiting Mindsets: Individual and collective beliefs that get in the way of progress

- What assumptions limit our potential and performance?
- Which beliefs make us feel powerless or stuck?
- What thoughts prevent us from moving forward?
- Which mindsets stop us from trying new things?

Liberating Mindsets: Individual and collective beliefs that enable the best version of your team

- What beliefs liberate our full potential?
- Which thoughts help us see opportunities in challenges?
- What assumptions enable us to take smart risks?
- Which mindsets make us feel capable and empowered?

Limiting Behaviors: Individual and collective conduct that harms relationships

- What practices go against our team's values or goals?
- Which behaviors create division and unnecessary friction?
- What actions should we call out or discourage?
- Which ways of working undermine trust or performance?

Liberating Behaviors: Individual and collective conduct that drives positive results

- What rituals or practices help us live out our values and achieve our goals?
- Which behaviors build trust and collaboration?
- What actions should we encourage and reward?
- Which ways of working bring out our best performance?

To make sense of the patterns, tackle one section at a time as a team and look for themes, contradictions, and connections. Cluster similar items and identify patterns.

For example, you might discover: "When deadlines approach, we feel anxious (limiting emotion), which reinforces our belief that we're always behind (limiting mindset), which leads to working in silos instead of asking for help (limiting behavior)."

Watch for contradictions between what you say you want and how you actually behave. For example: "We want to move quickly (liberating mindset), yet we become hesitant (limiting emotion) when risky ideas are presented and end up in analysis paralysis (limiting behavior)."

Select one to three key patterns or themes you want to improve.

Reframing the Tensions:

This is where the real work happens. For each of the selected patterns, ask: "How can we reframe this energy into Forward Talk?"

For example:

- Frustration about budget cuts → Motivation to become more efficient so the project won't suffer.

- Anxiety about new leadership → Curiosity to ask the leader about their expectations and leadership style. Share what you like about the team and ask what will improve or change.
- Overwhelmed by too many projects → Review all existing initiatives and prioritize and deprioritize accordingly.

Behaviors often shift mindsets and emotions. Taking action—having that conversation, making that decision, or saying goodbye to what changed—can transform how we think and feel about a situation. The goal is to redirect the existing energy toward productive outcomes rather than trying to eliminate tensions (our natural responses to change).

How (Not) to Sink Your Ship Canvas

Backward Talk Pattern It Addresses: Groupthink
Goal: Surface dangerous beliefs and behaviors before they sink an idea, project, or even the team

Teams often carry hidden beliefs that encourage them to make bad choices. Uncovering those beliefs will help you overcome the blame game that results when things go wrong. Most importantly, it will help you shift course and avoid hitting the iceberg next time.

How It Works:
Most groupthink disasters happen because teams operate on unexamined assumptions about their strengths, market position, or competitive advantages. When everyone believes the same comfortable myths—"Our customers love us and would never leave us," or

"Our technical advantage is permanent"—no one questions these beliefs until it's too late.

This canvas helps teams spot cracks in their hulls before they become serious problems. It guides you to uncover hidden risks, unchallenged assumptions, and external threats that could harm your team, project, or entire organization.

You will reflect on:

- What outdated beliefs are your team hanging on to?
- What regular behaviors might be steering you off course?
- What external forces are changing around you, and how can you adapt?

By systematically examining both internal threats (beliefs and behaviors) and external forces, your team will build awareness and prevent costly blind spots.

How to Apply It:

Work on the canvas in this order:

1: What External Forces Can Sink Our Ship?

Not everything is within a team's control. Market shifts, disruptive technologies, and regulatory changes can create unexpected waves that you must navigate to stay afloat. This section helps teams consider what's happening outside their walls and prepare for what's ahead, focusing their energy on what they can control.

Examples:

- "AI search is rapidly replacing traditional web browsers."
- "Clients expect 24/7 support as remote work becomes more pervasive."
- "Economic risk is reducing innovation budgets."

2: What Underlying Beliefs Can Sink Our Ship?

Sometimes, it's not what we do, but our underlying mindsets and assumptions that put us in danger. This section challenges teams to examine the "truths" they operate by and see if they're still useful.

Surface mindsets and assumptions about your people, company, competitors, and business model that could harm your success. These often include overconfidence about market position, underestimating competition, or believing your current approach will always work.

Examples:

- "We assume customers will always choose quality over price."
- "We think our employees are lazy, and if we let them work remotely, productivity will suffer."
- "We believe our brand loyalty is unshakeable."
- "We think our culture is strong and will continue attracting top talent."

How (Not) to Sink Your Ship©

Beliefs that could sink a project, idea, and even organization

What Are We Doing That Could Sink the Ship?
Identify behaviors that reflect our beliefs and might steer us off course. Are we stuck in outdated habits, ignoring risks, or overlooking new ideas?

How Can We Prevent Sinking Our Ship?
Ideate how to get rid of behaviors, norms, practices, and processes that are putting our ship at risk.

What Underlying Beliefs Can Sink Our Ship?
Describe mindsets and ideas about our company, our competition, and business model that could harm our business. Describe beliefs and assumptions about people that could sink our ship.

What External Forces Can Sink Our Ship?
Identify the societal, technological, and market shifts we can't control but must navigate to stay afloat.

3: What Are We Doing That Could Sink the Ship?

Every team has habits, decisions, and ways of working that might seem innocuous but could be harmful in the long run. This section helps teams identify self-inflicted risks before they cause real damage.

Identify behaviors that might derail your project, team, or organization. Look for patterns like avoiding difficult conversations, ignoring risks, or overloading new ideas without proper evaluation.

Examples:

- "We avoid giving constructive feedback."
- "We say yes to every opportunity."
- "We don't test assumptions before committing resources."

4: How Can We Prevent Sinking Our Ship?

This final section is about turning insight into action. Once you know the internal and external risks, you can develop strategies to course-correct, adapt, and build resilience.

Brainstorm ideas to eliminate problematic behaviors, norms, practices, and processes. Focus on specific actions that would address the risks identified in the previous quadrants.

Examples:

- Institute monthly assumption-testing sessions.
- Run a pre-mortem to identify why this initiative could fail.
- Create a red team that can challenge assumptions.

Facilitation Notes:

1. Allow participants to capture their notes first, and then facilitate a team discussion.

2. Encourage brutal honesty about vulnerabilities rather than trying to gloss over problems.
3. Focus on patterns and systems rather than assigning individual blame.
4. End with a commitment to specific prevention actions rather than just raising awareness.

Consent Decision-Making

Backward Talk Pattern It Addresses: Groupthink
Goal: Drive commitment when not everyone agrees with a decision

Most teams seek consensus, getting everyone to agree with the path forward, which leads to endless discussions that often result in subpar decisions. Consent decision-making[60] asks a different question: "Can you live with this decision?" rather than "Do you love this decision?" Unlike consensus, which wants everyone to say "yes," consent is about removing the objections—those who would say "no."

It's like choosing ice cream flavors for the whole team—you can't please everyone, but people can widen their tolerance by supporting a flavor that's not their top pick, as long as it's not one they dislike or can't eat.

How It Works:
Consent-based decisions are faster because they don't require everyone to be excited about every choice. While it's okay for people to disagree, at some point the team must give consent for the decision and support the path forward.

This approach moves beyond agree/disagree. It encourages team members to distinguish between their personal preferences ("my choice"), their range of tolerance ("I can live with it"), and their genuine objections ("no way"). By doing so, it reframes the conversation from a binary "yes" or "no" position.

The key insight here is that people who consent to decisions they didn't personally choose are more likely to support their implementation than people who superficially agreed to it. You're not looking for love—you're looking for commitment.

Consent-Facilitation Steps

	1 PROPOSAL	2 CLARIFYING QUESTIONS	3 REACTION ROUND
PROPOSER	Describes a tension and recommends a proposal to resolve it.	Answers questions with facts. No selling.	Listens.
TEAMMATES	Listen. No interruptions.	Ask questions to better understand the proposal.	React to the proposal.
FACILITATOR	Doesn't allow interruptions or side conversations.	Ensures people stick to questions (no opinions disguised as questions).	Lets people speak freely.

How to Apply It:

Follow this six-step process:

1. **Present the Proposal:** Anyone can start by describing a problem and proposing a solution. Always begin with "I propose we . . . " The clearer the proposal, the smoother the process.

2. **Clarifying Questions:** Team members ask questions to understand the proposal—not to challenge or improve it, just to clarify. The proposer answers each question; it's okay to say, "Not specified" or "I don't know yet." No reactions or opinions are allowed in this round, and a facilitator ensures that people are not sharing opinions disguised as questions. This is a moment to improve understanding—teams often jump into judgment without really understanding the solution they're criticizing.

	4 RESTATE PROPOSAL	5 OBJECTION ROUND	6 RATIFICATION
PROPOSER	Clarifies or amends the proposal (optional).	Listens.	Amends proposal.
TEAMMATES	Listen. No interruptions.	Consent or object based on: Will this proposal move the team backward or create irreparable harm?	Commit to action.
FACILITATOR	No discussion allowed.	Ensures objections are: objective, fact-based, real, and not future tensions.	Captures agreements.

3. **Reaction Round:** One by one, each person shares their reaction to the proposal. The proposer just listens. Others can speak freely, share perspectives, or even suggest improvements. No discussion or responses—the facilitator just captures all reactions.

4. **Restate Proposal:** The proposer can choose to amend the proposal based on questions and reactions, or they can keep it as originally stated. This isn't about seeking consensus but tapping into collective wisdom. We frequently miss information or perspectives when making a decision. The proposer can improve their proposal based on people's feedback.
5. **Objection Round:** The facilitator asks each person, "Do you see any reasons why adopting this proposal would cause harm or move us backward?" This is the acid test. Objections must be objective, based on present facts rather than being driven by personal preferences or what might happen ten years from now. Valid objections can block the decision.
6. **Integration:** If objections surface, the proposer adjusts the proposal to address them. Continue objection rounds until a solution emerges free of valid objections, or the proposer withdraws the proposal.

The goal is to end with everyone giving consent to the proposer, which requires some back and forth between team members and, most importantly, positive intent. If you play hardball, your colleagues will pay you back when you're in the hot seat.

Consent helps teams move forward with decisions everyone can commit to, even if not everyone loves them.

Regain Your Power Canvas

Backward Talk Pattern It Addresses: Blame

Goal: Shift from "blaming what you can't control" to owning what you can

In most organizations, people choose not to act because of (perceived) lack of authority, resources, or control. They get stuck in blame cycles, complaining about the things they don't have or why others have more than they do. Having worked with hundreds of teams, I can tell you this: I've never seen a single one that thought it had more budget or resources than it needed. When we focus on what we lack—when we compare ourselves to other teams—we always end up disappointed, or even powerless.

The "Regain Your Power Canvas" will help increase your impact by reframing the conversation. Rather than focusing on what you can't control, flip the situation and reclaim your power.

Regain Your Power Canvas©

Focus on what you can control

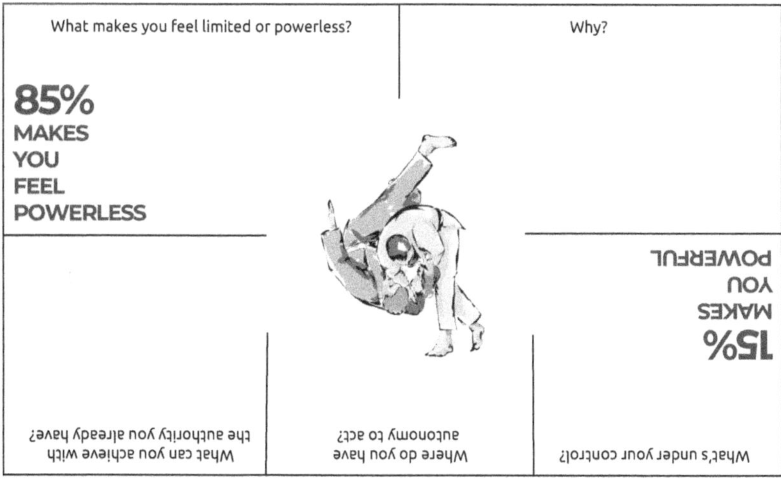

How It Works:

When people feel powerless, they blame forces beyond their control—leadership decisions, market conditions, and other departments. This blame pattern becomes a mental trap that keeps teams stuck. This canvas uses a simple reframe: Instead of focusing on the 85 percent you can't control, redirect energy toward the 15 percent you can influence.

You have to literally flip the canvas to reframe the focus. This mental shift embodies the principles of judo: Instead of fighting the weight of your opponent (what you can't control), use that energy to your advantage. By focusing on what you can act on, you move from feeling powerless to powerful.

How to Apply It:

Start by filling out the "85 percent that makes you feel powerless." Ask your team to list everything that makes them feel limited—one idea per sticky note. For example, competitors' prices that can't be matched, not being able to promote or hire people, or a lack of senior management support. Have team members reflect on why these things frustrate them, both emotionally and practically.

Now comes the flip: Physically turn the canvas upside down so "15 percent makes you powerful" is now at the top. Ask team members to list everything under their control, no matter how small. Remind them to capture every bit of autonomy they have. For instance, how we respond to setbacks, setting team-specific priorities and deadlines, leaning on strong collaboration and the desire to help each other, or demonstrating a problem-solving mentality are all examples of choices that team members make every day.

Next, identify areas where your team has the freedom to act. Have the team acknowledge that they have more power than they usually believe—authority they're not using, relationships they haven't leveraged, and skills they haven't applied.

Finally, ask participants to focus on identifying opportunities to do more with that power. What can you achieve with what you already have? What small actions could create momentum?

The physical flip is more than a metaphor; it's a reminder of how reframing a conversation can move your team from feeling powerless to powerful.

Exercise Quick Reference

You now have ten strategic solutions for transforming Backward Talk into Forward Talk. Here's a quick recap to help you choose where to start based on your team's specific challenges and goals.

To make it easier, each solution is marked with a level of facilitation support:

- **Not Needed:** Teams can implement these straightforward processes on their own
- **Recommended:** Skilled facilitation can accelerate the process and promote deep insights
- **Strongly Recommended:** Requires an expert facilitator familiar with the technique and implementation challenges

Exercise	Backward Pattern	Goal	Expert Facilitation
Reframing Mindsets			
Recovering Team Agency	Avoidance	Shift from "difficult conversations never work for us" to "we can handle them when conditions are right"	Recommended
The Three Perspectives	Groupthink	Shift from "challenging ideas is disloyal" to "systematic challenge strengthens decisions"	Recommended
Rapid Recovery from Mistakes	Blame	Shift from "hiding mistakes and dwelling on them" to "recovering quickly and applying lessons"	Not Needed
The Conversational Observer	All Patterns	Shift from "operating unconsciously" to "noticing our communication patterns"	Not Needed
Delivering Bad News	Blame	Shift from "messengers get shot" to "truth-telling is protected"	Not Needed

Exercise	Backward Pattern	Goal	Expert Facilitation
Forward Talk Tools			
The Stinky Fish	Avoidance	Surface avoided issues to maintain harmony	Strongly Recommended
Cultural Tensions Canvas	Groupthink	Shift from "avoiding tensions" to "using tensions as building blocks"	Strongly Recommended
How (Not) to Sink Your Ship Canvas	Groupthink	Surface dangerous beliefs and behaviors before they create groupthink disasters	Recommended
Consent Decision-Making	Groupthink	Drive commitment when not everyone agrees with a decision	Recommended
Regain Your Power Canvas	Blame	Shift from "blaming what we can't control" to "owning what we can control"	Recommended

These strategic solutions can transform how your team approaches difficult conversations, but only if they become habits rather than one-time interventions. You don't need to adopt all of them to see real change.

In the next chapter, you'll learn how to prevent conversational debt from building up again so your progress sticks.

CHAPTER 19

Preventing Future Debt

"We don't rise to the level of our goals; we fall to the level of our systems."

—James Clear

Now that you've learned how to reframe conversations in the moment and to apply the various Forward Talk tools, let's move into how to prevent future debt from piling up. Without prevention habits, your team could fall back to where it started.

In this chapter, I'll discuss how to build regular, repeatable habits that protect your team from accumulating conversational debt before it starts.

When deadlines loom or stress mounts, teams default to whatever feels familiar—avoiding difficult conversations, rushing to false consensus, or falling into blame cycles. All your progress evaporates because doing things right feels optional when urgency strikes.

Don't approach Forward Talk like a New Year's resolution—with lots of enthusiasm at the outset, then gradual abandonment when real life kicks in. Instead, treat it like exercising regularly: a nonnegotiable habit woven into your lifestyle.

You've learned the exercises—now it's time to build resilience through frequency to create lasting change, making these tools part of your culture.

The good news is that building conversational immunity isn't about complex tracking systems or formal processes. It's about simple habits that make Forward Talk natural, preventing conversational debt from piling up.

Make Solutions Stick

So, where do you start? Begin by making your solutions stick. Sustainable change happens when you embed new practices into existing rhythms rather than treating them as special events.

Embed Tools in Ongoing Practices

Rather than adding new meetings to the calendar, weave Forward Talk into the conversations your team is already having.

One client implemented a Stinky Fish session into their bimonthly team review. Another opens weekly meetings with "Any stinky fish we need to discuss?" These rituals turn the tool into a regular practice, not a one-off activity.

You can also use the Three Perspectives exercise regularly for idea selection, decision-making, or other situations where groupthink is a threat. Having different members regularly play the Challenger, Explorer, and Skeptic roles reminds everyone of the importance of integrating multiple points of view.

Frequency transforms intervention tools into immunity builders. What starts as a solution to an issue becomes a tool of early detection and prevention.

Build on What Works

Identify where your team naturally communicates well, then transfer those skills to challenging areas.

For example, Consent Decision-Making helps teams separate understanding from reaction—first clarify what's being proposed, then respond with your perspective. You can apply this same principle to customer conversations: Listen fully to understand their concerns before jumping to solutions or defenses.

If your team handles technical debates effectively by focusing on systemic issues rather than symptoms, apply that same approach for strategy discussions. Or if you're excellent at reframing your customers' objections when they focus on what's not working or what they can't control, use those same reframing skills when colleagues complain about internal processes or other limitations.

When you build on what's already working, Forward Talk becomes second nature, not just another tool. This approach fosters a continuous improvement mindset around how your team communicates.

Catch Debt Early

Preventing conversational debt requires developing early warning systems to detect both early signals and growing structural problems.

The Future Regret Test

Before avoiding a problematic topic, ask your team: "Ten years from now, will we regret staying silent about this more than speaking up, even if the conversation doesn't go perfectly?"

This question is a powerful call to action. It reminds teams that the long-term cost of silence usually outweighs the short-term discomfort of speaking up.

Remember that we tend to regret what we didn't do twice as much as what we did—that deteriorating client relationship, the strategy assumption that feels wrong, the team dynamic that's affecting everyone, but nobody mentions—each avoided conversation accumulates interest on the debt.

Monthly Debt Check-Ins

Turn debt detection into a prevention habit using the diagnostic questions from Chapters 8, 9, and 10:

- **Alignment Debt:** "Can everyone name our top three organizational priorities without hesitation?" "Is there consistency between the behaviors we say we value and what we reward?"
- **Belonging Debt:** "Are diverse perspectives genuinely explored, not just acknowledged?" "Do people regularly give each other honest feedback, not just praise?"
- **Collaboration Debt:** "Are people clear on how decisions are made and who has the authority to make them?" "Does important information reach the right people without overwhelming everyone else?"

If the same issues keep surfacing repeatedly without resolution, that's a sign of accumulating interest. Each month of avoidance makes the eventual conversation more expensive and more difficult.

Rotate Monitoring Responsibility

Debt detection shouldn't fall solely on the leader. But when everyone's responsible, often no one takes action since individuals assume that others will speak up. (You can read more about the Bystander Effect in Chapter 13.)

Instead, assign rotating roles for responsibility—one person tracks alignment issues this month, another watches for belonging debt, and a third monitors collaboration problems.

When it's everyone's job but someone's turn, things don't get missed.

Build Conversational Resilience

Strong teams don't just prevent conversational debt; they build conversational resilience. They adapt faster by surfacing issues before they compound. They innovate better because diverse perspectives are genuinely welcomed. They execute more effectively because alignment is real rather than assumed.

Scale What Works

Pay attention to which Forward Talk practices your team naturally adopts, or which consistently delivers better results, and double down on those.

For example, Consent Decision-Making is especially effective for recurring, high-risk decisions that typically drain energy, such as quarterly priorities, budget allocation, or establishing hiring criteria. However, you don't have to limit this technique to those occasions. Once your team members master the consent approach, it becomes second nature. Expand its application and use it to tackle regular, low-complexity decisions.

The path to Forward Talk isn't rigid, but organic. Start with small, quick wins and then build momentum toward more structural transformations.

Understand the Principles of Progress

Building conversational resilience follows predictable patterns:

- **Practice makes permanent, not perfect.** The goal isn't flawless conversations but consistent improvement. Each difficult conversation builds your team's capacity to have the next one.
- **Some tools yield quicker results than others.** Pattern recognition tools like the Future Regret Test, discussed earlier, can provide immediate value. Deeper interventions, like the Cultural Tensions Canvas, require more time but can transform how teams handle change. And consider that what works well for one team might not work for yours.
- **Expect resistance before adoption.** New approaches feel awkward initially, and teams might resist tools that challenge comfortable patterns. But this resistance signals you're addressing real issues, not just symptoms. Name the discomfort and invite curiosity rather than simply pushing through it.
- **Progress isn't linear.** Teams advance, then slide back under pressure, then advance again. The regression doesn't erase progress—it reveals where habits need strengthening.

Understanding these patterns helps your team stay grounded through the ups and downs of change and be better prepared for what comes next.

Turn Prevention into Practice

Forward Talk works like building muscle memory—it develops through repetition, not one-time training sessions. And don't forget that progress happens faster when teams enjoy the process! Most workplace issues aren't life-or-death problems, yet teams treat them as such. A bit of levity reminds everyone that we're only human, and makes difficult conversations feel less intimidating and more memorable.

The prevention habits you build today determine whether your team thrives or struggles with future challenges. The earlier you start and the more consistent you are, the greater your advantage compounds over time.

In the next chapter, you'll explore the Forward Talk Canvas to help your team identify which tools it needs the most, as well as when to use them. Instead of trying everything at once, you'll become more intentional about which tools work best for your team.

CHAPTER 20

The Forward Talk Canvas

In the previous chapters, we explored different ways to put Forward Talk into action, from reframing conversations in the moment to building strategic Forward Talk practices to preventing conversational debt. The Breaking the Conversational Loop Canvas (Chapter 6) helped you recognize Backward Talk patterns. The Conversational Debt Spiral Canvas (Chapter 12) showed you where your team gets stuck and why. Now it's time to bring it all together with the third canvas in the series: the Forward Talk Canvas. This final canvas is about navigating a path forward together. It's a practical tool for addressing specific conversations and recurring patterns as a team.

To me, courageous conversations feel like whitewater rafting. They're unpredictable, intense, and sometimes risky—but once you've made it to the other side, you never regret the experience. That's why this canvas is built around the whitewater metaphor.

Most teams expect collaboration to feel like paddling on smooth, steady rivers—everyone working in sync, moving in one direction, while being in total control. This illusion makes any disruption or tension—rapids—feel temporary, as if things will always return to normal, calm waters.

But here's the truth: The rapids never really stop appearing. There's always another difficult topic, another challenging conversation, or another moment when the team must navigate through turbulent waters together. A calm river is the exception, not the rule. The more you practice navigating whitewater, the less intimidating it becomes.

In rivers, whitewater forms when rocks, sharp turns, or sudden drops disrupt the flow. The result is a mix of resistance, speed, and unpredictability. Navigating these rapids is fast and chaotic, but it's also thrilling. Teams feel the same way when they face difficult conversations. Paddle too slowly, and you spin. Freeze, and you flip. Whitewater is not an obstacle—it's the path forward. And it demands full participation. There are no passengers in conversational rapids. Success requires coordination, reading the water, and steering toward your destination while avoiding the rocks that could flip over your boat. Your team must learn to navigate—not avoid—courageous conversations.

The turbulence is where the magic happens.

Though whitewater feels chaotic, it's mainly composed of patterns. If you stop and observe a river, you can find some structure within the chaos. The same applies to difficult conversations—even though they may seem daunting, they follow predictable patterns that teams can learn to look for.

Canvas Structure

The Forward Talk Canvas contains six key elements that help you map your team's navigation plan, organized in three sections:

1. Spot the Trouble:
   - **Avoidance:** This is the starting point—the unresolved issues or patterns your team needs to address.
   - **Whitewater:** These are the risks that make this conversation feel dangerous, like the things we can't control or that we fear.
2. Identify the Risks:
   - **Blame:** Finger-pointing could get your team stuck.
   - **Groupthink:** Superficial agreement could capsize the conversation.
3. Navigate Together:
   - **Forward Talk:** Create a team game plan using Courage, Perspective, and Responsibility.
   - **Success:** How you'll know you've successfully navigated this conversation.

Forward Talk Canvas©
Navigating courageous conversations

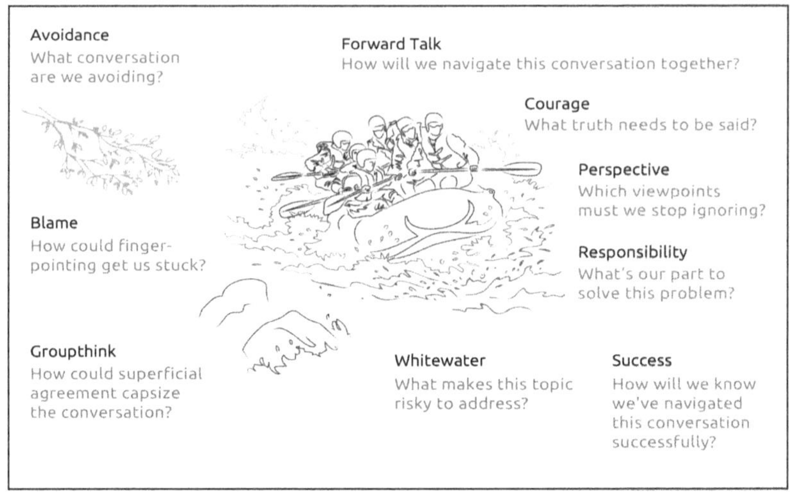

Using the Canvas

Step 1: Define the Context

Frame this as navigation planning for a specific difficult conversation your team needs to have. Like whitewater rafting, you can't avoid the turbulence—you have to move through it together.

Decide whether you're addressing a specific unresolved issue (such as conflicting priorities, performance problems, or strategic disagreements) or broader conversational patterns. Focusing on specific issues tends to work better when there's a clear problem affecting team performance.

Step 2: Identify the Starting Point

Pinpoint the unresolved issue your team needs to address. Ask: "What conversation are we avoiding?"

Examples include: Conflicting priorities that paralyze and stall decision-making, a reorganization that only leadership supports, performance issues everyone sees but no one names and discusses, or a friendly culture that prioritizes and values consensus over speed.

Have team members write down their thoughts individually, then share. Use the team's perspective to identify the most critical issue to focus on.

Step 3: Codify the Whitewater

Identify the fears and risks associated with addressing this issue. Ask: "What makes this topic feel risky to bring up?"

Capture specific concerns, such as the fear of conflict escalation, damaging relationships, appearing disloyal, presenting issues that may not be solvable, or risking making things worse.

Remember, you are seeking to surface these fears to explain why teams are avoiding the conversation, not whether the fears are rational or justified.

Step 4: Identify Backward Talk Patterns

Map the two Backward Talk patterns that could get your team stuck in the rapids or capsize the conversation:

Blame: "How could finger-pointing get us stuck?"

Identify specific blame triggers related to your issue that could derail productive dialogue—such as what's happening now or what might happen.

Groupthink: "How could superficial agreement capsize the conversation?"

Spot the moments when the team might default to agreement too quickly, avoiding real disagreement or skipping over diverse perspectives.

Step 5: Build Forward Talk Capacity

Design how your team will coordinate using the three CPR elements—Courage, Perspective, and Responsibility—by asking, "How will we navigate this conversation together?"

Courage: "What truth needs to be said?"

Commit to naming real issues, not just symptoms. Focus on what needs to be spoken directly about this specific topic. Capture ideas for breaking the silence and holding one another accountable for speaking up. Focus both on individual and collective courage.

Perspective: "Which viewpoints must we stop ignoring?"

Aim to not just include different viewpoints—be open to changing your mind. Identify which perspectives are essential to this conversation, and which are missing, dismissed, or silenced.

Responsibility: "What's our part in solving this problem?"

Commit to owning your part in the solution instead of blaming others. Focus on how each team member will contribute to the resolution. This requires a mix of both individual and collective ownership.

Step 6: Define Success

Clarify what success looks like so your team knows when the conversation has been navigated well. Ask: "How will we know we've navigated this conversation successfully?"

Examples of success include:

- The real issue gets addressed, not just the symptoms.
- People share concerns during the meeting, not after.
- The team reaches a genuine resolution, not forced agreement.
- Everyone commits to the path forward, even those who initially disagreed.

Before moving on, ask your team: "What's one conversation your team has been avoiding that could benefit from this canvas? What will it feel like to be on the other side of this conversation?" Paint that picture together. That shared image of success can become your compass in the chaos.

The Forward Talk Canvas isn't a one-and-done tool. You can use it for specific difficult topics your team needs to address or to improve your general conversational patterns. The more you use it, the better you become at navigating whitewater—and you may even enjoy the thrill. Crossing the rapids feels risky at first, but once you go through them, you realize it's actually safer on the other side. The more you practice the power of Forward Talk, the more rewarding and better the collaboration will become.

PART IV RECAP

Move Forward

In Summary:

Reframing conversations will help your team get unstuck. You shift energy from Backward Talk patterns to Forward Talk progress. This happens in three ways: Practice strategic solutions until they become habits, build a culture of courageous conversations, and stop negative patterns before they pile up.

Team conversations are unpredictable and messy. Pick tools that fit your context, but don't play it safe.

Key Takeaways:

- Reframing conversations helps you turn objections into exploration.
- Prepare for hard talks. Identify what you're avoiding, what could go wrong, and how you'll handle it with CPR.
- To build a Forward Talk culture, you need more than tools. Build partnerships and communities that support courageous conversations.
- Sustain small, repeatable habits to stop conversational debt from piling up again.
- Progress feels messy before it gets clear. Keep going.

The Only Path Is Forward

You deserve more than a safe space where you can speak up. You deserve to reclaim the voice you've been surrendering and to stop giving away your power in the conversations that matter most. You deserve a team that's not afraid to address issues openly—that wants to move forward, not stay stuck in the past.

As we end this journey together, you now have a framework to make that vision real. You understand how conversational debt accumulates from poorly managed or avoided conversations. You can recognize the three destructive patterns—Blame, Avoidance, and Groupthink—that trap teams in vicious loops. And you know that Forward Talk provides a way out: the road to resolution, moving into the future.

Those frustrating meetings that seemed to go nowhere? You now see them as predictable roundabouts with clear exits. The conversations you used to dread? You now understand that the cost of avoiding them exceeds the risks of having them.

You're no longer at the mercy of dysfunctional team patterns—you now know how to redirect them. The courage you were looking for was already there. And rather than waiting for someone to create the perfect conditions, you now have the tools to break Backward Talk patterns and move forward.

You're probably already thinking about the obstacles ahead: What if you don't have a title with the authority to introduce new approaches? What if you try to redirect a blame session and it backfires? What if your team rolls their eyes at anything that sounds like a framework? What if you ask, "What conversation are we avoiding?" and the room goes silent—or, worse, erupts into conflict you can't handle?

These are all valid concerns, but here's what's certain: Doing nothing will make things worse—the conversational debt will keep compounding, the patterns will keep repeating, and the frustration will keep building. If you don't intervene, you risk surrendering not just your voice but your courage, perspective, and responsibility.

Move from Words to Action

Now it's your turn.

Begin where you can. Start small, with a couple of colleagues who are also tired of meetings that go nowhere. Try one conversational reframe in the moment—just once. Own your part in one problem instead of pointing fingers. Ask one genuine question when everyone's rushing to agree just so they can move on.

You don't need to convince everyone—start with one conversation at a time. You started reading this book probably because something wasn't working in your team's conversations. Now, you're equipped with a shared language, a practical framework, and the courage to take action. Every time you choose courage over comfort, you give others permission to do the same. Your willingness to address real issues signals that speaking up can change things for the better. The issues you used to avoid become opportunities to practice what you've learned.

That colleague who never seems to listen? Use it as a chance to model curiosity. The project retrospective that always turns into a blame session? Invite a few colleagues to help you explore what's wrong with the system—not just the symptoms. The strategy meeting where everyone nods but no one's really aligned? Ask what's missing or what doubts people are holding back.

As you head into the future with Forward Talk, remember that progress is rarely linear. Some days, you'll successfully retire a destructive pattern; other days, you'll feel like you're talking to a wall. Both experiences are valuable. The courage you build during difficult moments creates the capacity for accelerating momentum.

Model the conversations you want to have. Pass on what you've learned. Share what worked and what didn't. Try new methods and adapt them to your team's challenges. Forward Talk isn't about using templates or following scripts, but about reframing conversations to get teams unstuck.

Forward Talk doesn't end here. The conversations that matter most are still ahead of you. If you want to keep learning, connect with others, or share how these ideas are taking shape in your team, visit gustavorazzetti.com. You'll find more resources, stories, and support for your team.

Thank you for trusting me along the journey. Here's to the conversations that matter, the courage to have them, and the progress you deserve.

Glossary of Key Terms

This glossary provides quick reference to key concepts from Forward Talk. For detailed explanations and applications, refer to the relevant chapters.

Avoidance: One of the three Backward Talk patterns. Teams get stuck in silence and inaction by choosing not to address issues, either hoping problems will resolve themselves or fearing the consequences of speaking up. This creates temporary comfort at the expense of long-term progress.

Backward Talk: The three conversational patterns that get teams stuck: Avoidance (silence), Blame (finger-pointing), and Groupthink (fake agreements). This is the opposite of Forward Talk—focusing on symptoms rather than root causes, and on past problems rather than solutions.

Belonging Debt: The cost that builds when teams prioritize artificial harmony over authentic dialogue. People withhold concerns, soften feedback, and avoid challenging popular ideas to maintain cohesion, ultimately weakening both relationships and outcomes.

Blame: One of the three Backward Talk patterns. Teams get stuck in the past and become defensive because they focus on finding fault rather than solving problems. While it may feel like issues are being addressed, blame creates cycles of finger-pointing that harm trust.

Bystander Effect: A psychological phenomenon where the presence of others makes individuals less likely to intervene in emergencies. In teams, this manifests as diffusion of responsibility. When everyone is responsible for speaking up, no one feels compelled to act.

Collaboration Debt: The cost that builds when teams fail to reach resolution. Decisions are never final, meetings end by scheduling another meeting, and simple disagreements transform into endless discussions while opportunities slip away.

Conversational Agency: The power to influence outcomes by regaining your voice in team conversations. Most people surrender their power, voice, and judgment to others or external circumstances, becoming passive participants rather than active contributors.

Conversational Debt: The mounting cost of crucial conversations that teams avoid or mismanage. Like financial debt, it starts small and compounds over time, resulting in much greater costs than the discomfort teams sought to avoid.

CPR Framework: The foundation of the Forward Talk model based on three interventions that move teams from Backward Talk patterns to meaningful dialogue: *Courage* (speaking up instead of surrendering to silence), *Perspective* (sharing views instead of surrendering judgment to social pressure), and *Responsibility* (understanding systemic issues instead of surrendering to blame).

Drama Triangle: A psychological model that describes three powerless roles team members unconsciously play: Hero, Victim, and Villain. Each role reinforces each other, driving Backward Talk. Victims avoid action, Villains attack people instead of problems, and Heroes rush to fix everything. These roles create a vicious cycle that traps teams in endless drama.

Forward Talk: A practical approach to team conversations that builds both individual and collective capacity. It's the discipline of having conversations that accomplish two things: 1) *Address the real issue* (tackle the root cause, not symptoms, excuses, or side topics), and 2) *Future Focus* (what needs to happen next to find resolution, rather than dwelling on what went wrong). Forward Talk is the antidote to the three patterns that keep teams stuck: avoidance, blame, and groupthink.

Forward Talk Matrix: Built on two essential dimensions that create four conversational zones: Time Orientation (past vs. future) and Issue

Engagement (surface vs. deep engagement). Only Forward Talk leads to meaningful action by addressing real issues with future focus. The other three zones (blame, avoidance, and groupthink) lead to Backward Talk.

Forward Talk Journey: The five milestones teams navigate to move from avoidance to commitment: Initiate the Talk, Keep an Open Mind, Explore the Root Cause, Generate Solutions, and Commit to Action.

Groupthink: One of the three Backward Talk patterns. Teams create superficial alignment and miss important perspectives by maintaining a facade of harmony while avoiding real issues. This leads to both fake alignment that falls apart during implementation and mediocre decisions that prioritize comfort over effectiveness.

Pointlessness Paradox: The phenomenon where people stop speaking up or avoid difficult conversations when they believe nothing will change or that people won't change. This sense of futility, not fear, is the primary reason why people avoid conversations, regardless of how safe their culture seems to be.

Psychological Safety Bubble: An overprotective approach that wrongly treats safety as a prerequisite for courageous conversations. Instead of promoting a courageous space, people wait for the perfect conditions to never materialize. This postpones meaningful conversations while conversational debt continues to accumulate. People misuse "this is not safe" as an excuse for not participating, which paradoxically worsens the conditions they're waiting to improve.

Vulnerability Loop: The contagious effect that occurs when one person's social risk encourages others to reciprocate, creating a chain reaction of vulnerable behavior. The loop hinges on the second person's response. Their willingness to reciprocate vulnerability determines whether the loop continues or breaks.

The Forward Talk System: Visual Recap

We've covered a lot together—from conversational roundabouts to Drama Triangles. So, here's a friendly overview to help you keep track. The visual shows you the entire Forward Talk system at a glance. It captures how everything works and when to use which canvases or tools.

Use it to define your path or track your progress. Share it with a colleague who hasn't read the book to explain the framework. Use it when planning your next intervention. Revisit it to recognize how seemingly separate issues—like avoidance, conversational debt, or surrendering power—are all interconnected.

Keep this diagram visible. Share it with your colleagues. Remember, transforming conversations is both science and art. The framework provides the structure and tools, but you need to make it work for your team. Experiment, adapt it, and let the magic happen.

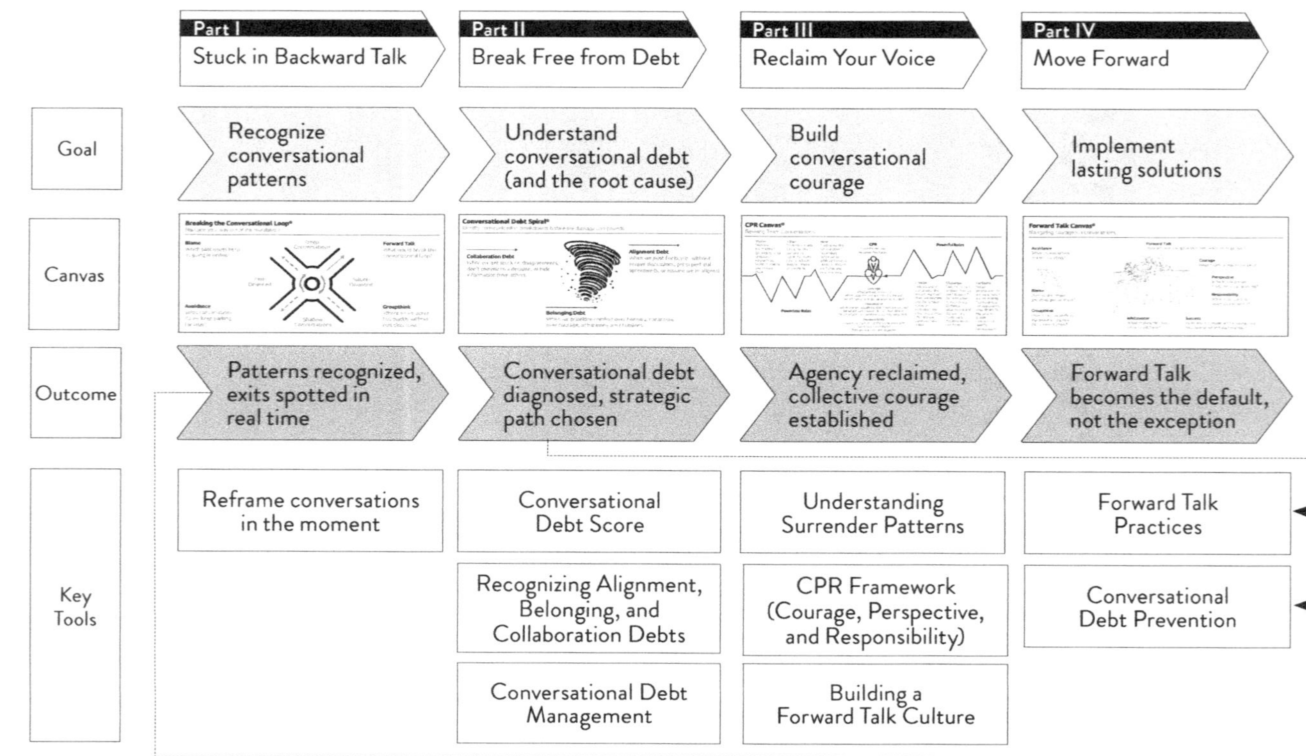
Forward Talk System—Transform Your Team's Conversations
Part I
Stuck in Backward Talk
Part II
Break Free from Debt
Part III
Reclaim Your Voice
Part IV
Move Forward
Goal
Recognize conversational patterns
Understand conversational debt (and the root cause)
Build conversational courage
Implement lasting solutions
Canvas
Outcome
Patterns recognized, exits spotted in real time
Conversational debt diagnosed, strategic path chosen
Agency reclaimed, collective courage established
Forward Talk becomes the default, not the exception
Key Tools
Reframe conversations in the moment
Conversational Debt Score
Recognizing Alignment, Belonging, and Collaboration Debts
Conversational Debt Management
Understanding Surrender Patterns
CPR Framework (Courage, Perspective, and Responsibility)
Building a Forward Talk Culture
Forward Talk Practices
Conversational Debt Prevention

Before You Finish

You now know how to spot what's stopping your team from having better conversations—and how to fix it.

Ready to use Forward Talk with your team? Start here:

- Take the quiz to identify your team's conversational debt
- Use the templates to surface difficult topics
- Check the resources to choose where to start

Go to gustavorazzetti.com/forward-talk-tools
or scan the QR code below.

Acknowledgments

First, thank YOU for reading this book. You're here because you want to improve your team conversations. Maybe you have the courage but need better tools. Maybe your team is stuck. Maybe you're the one holding back. Or maybe you're ready to challenge groupthink and stop going in circles. Whatever brings you here, thank you for trusting me with something so important.

This book was shaped by many people. *Forward Talk* takes courage, and this book exists because of courage—from people who believed in the idea early, challenged my thinking, and supported me when my courage wasn't enough.

To my wife, **Moira**—thank you for your patience and company. For all the hours I spent writing, for listening to half-baked ideas, for the late nights and early mornings, and for encouraging me to keep going. Most of all, thank you for being courageous—in everything you do.

To my **beta readers**—thank you for challenging my ideas and being so generous with your time. Your feedback made this book sharper, clearer, and more grounded.

Pete Armstrong, Ewa Hutmacher, Paul O'Kelly, Sarah Walsh, Andrew O'Hearn, Silvina Cendra, Emanuele Mazzanti, Hyla Pollak, Michelle Wendt, Zora Artis, Marco Vianello, Astha Lagoo, Steve Urquhart, Michelle Choate, and Bernie Thorpe.

To **Myriam Hadnes**, thank you for being my writing sparring partner. Writing a book can be lonely; you made it less so.

To my early editors, **Bonnie Jaynem** and **Jess Lomas**, thank you for reviewing all my early drafts and helping me see what needed to go.

To the **Ideapress Publishing team**, thank you for guiding this book from rough draft to finished product. Your experience, wisdom, and dedication made a real difference.

Rohit Bhargava, Lynnette McCurdy, Kameron Bryant-Sergejev, Megan Wheeler, Allison Griffith, Athena Potkovic, and Chhavi Arya Bhargava.

To the team at **Simon & Schuster**, thank you for believing in this book and helping bring it into the world.

To my broader community—my readers, supporters, workshop participants, and LinkedIn connections—thank you for being part of this journey. Your questions, feedback, and encouragement shaped this book more than you know. Many of the ideas here came from real conversations with you.

And finally, to my clients, for the honor of helping you as a facilitator. Some of you tried these ideas when they were brand new. You invited me into difficult, personal conversations—many of them messy and uncomfortable. You trusted me, even when we weren't sure how things would turn out. We made it through together. Thank you for letting me challenge you and for being so fearless.

Endnotes

Introduction

1 Gustavo Razzetti, “Facilitation: The Most Underrated Leadership Skill,” Demystify Culture (Substack), November 9, 2025, https://think.fearlessculture.design/p/leaders-are-facilitators-of-conversations.

PART I: Stuck in Backward Talk

Chapter 1: When Talking Becomes Pointless

2 Jordan Christiansen, “Costly Conversations: How Lack of Communication Is Costing Organizations Thousands in Revenue,” Crucial Learning, February 3, 2022, https://cruciallearning.com/press/costly-conversations-how-lack-of-communication-is-costing-organizations-thousands-in-revenue/.

3 CPP Global Human Capital Report, CPP, July 2008, https://img.en25.com/Web/CPP/Conflict_report.pdf.

4 Emma Sarro and Ryan Curl, “From Breakdown to Breakthrough: Managing Threat Response in the Workplace,” in Your Brain at Work, produced by NeuroLeadership Institute, podcast, 53:55, https://neuroleadership.com/podcast/managing-threat-response.

5 David Maxfield, “How a Culture of Silence Eats Away at Your Company,” *Harvard Business Review*, December 7, 2016, https://hbr.org/2016/12/how-a-culture-of-silence-eats-away-at-your-company.

6 David Maxfield et al., “Silence Kills: The Seven Crucial Conversations for Healthcare,” Crucial Learning, 2005, https://vitalsmarts.widen.net/s/jfhgnsltfk/research---silence-kills.

7 Joseph Grenny and David Maxfield, “Five Crucial Conversations That Drive Workplace Safety, The Campbell Institute, 2011, https://www.thecampbellinstitute.org/wp-content/uploads/2017/07/Grenny-Maxfield_0811Z.pdf.

Chapter 2: The Forward Talk Model

8 Anita Williams Woolley et al., "Evidence for a Collective Intelligence Factor in the Performance of Human Groups," *Science* 330, 6004 (2010): 686–88, doi:10.1126/science.1193147.

9 Brené Brown, *The Gifts of Imperfection: Let Go of Who You Think You're Supposed to Be and Embrace Who You Are* (Hazelden Publishing, 2022).

10 Kendra Cherry, "How Groupthink Impacts Our Behavior," Verywell Mind, updated September 23, 2025, https://www.verywellmind.com/what-is-groupthink-2795213.

11 Kathleen M. Eisenhardt et al., "How Management Teams Can Have a Good Fight," *Harvard Business Review*, July–August 1997, https://hbr.org/1997/07/how-management-teams-can-have-a-good-fight.

Chapter 3: Conversational Debt

12 "The ABCs of Culture," Fearless Culture, accessed November 17, 2025, https://think.fearlessculture.design/p/how-to-make-culture-tangible-and.

Chapter 4: From Avoidance to Commitment

13 "Culture Design Masterclass," Fearless Culture, accessed February 9, 2026, https://www.fearlessculture.design/services-training/culture-design-masterclass.

Part II: Break Free from Debt
Chapter 7: The Cost of Silence

14 Josh Wright, "What Is the Power of Regret? A Conversation with Daniel Pink," *Behavioral Scientist*, December 13, 2022, https://behavioralscientist.org/what-is-the-power-of-regret-a-conversation-with-daniel-pink/.

15 Future Ready Leadership with Jacob Morgan, "Four Types of Regrets by Dan Pink," YouTube video, 6:28, October 27, 2022, https://www.youtube.com/watch?v=tlGIRzSqhlg.

Chapter 8: The Illusion of Alignment

16 Rebecca Homkes, "The Illusion of Alignment: Why Your Strategy Execution Is Failing," Chief Executive, March 12, 2024, https://chiefexecutive.net/the-illusion-of-alignment-why-your-strategy-execution-is-failing/.

17 "Why Senior Managers Can't Name Their Firms' Top Priorities," London Business School, December 7, 2015, https://www.london.edu/news/two-thirds-of-senior-managers-cant-name-their-firms-top-priorities.

18 Suzanne Choney, "Obama Gets to Keep His BlackBerry," NBC News, January 22, 2009, https://www.nbcnews.com/id/wbna28780205.

19 Justine Brown, "Why Businesses Fell Out of Love with BlackBerry," TechTarget, CIO Dive, October 10, 2016, https://www.ciodive.com/news/blackberry-businesses-stopped-using/427866/.

20 "Four Ways to Put Your Purpose to Work in 2021," Ernst & Young Global Limited, November 10, 2020, https://www.ey.com/en_in/insights/long-term-value/four-ways-to-put-your-purpose-to-work-in-2021.

21 "The Last Thing We Need Right Now Is a Vision Statement," *Farnam Street* (blog), accessed February 10, 2026, https://fs.blog/vision-statement/.

22 Denise McClain and Ryan Pendell, "Why Trust in Leaders Is Faltering and How to Gain It Back," Gallup Workplace, April 16, 2023, https://www.gallup.com/workplace/473738/why-trust-leaders-faltering-gain-back.aspx.

Chapter 9: The Tyranny of Harmony

23 "Transform Your Workplace with the Culture Design Canvas©," Fearless Culture, accessed February 10, 2026, https://www.fearlessculture.design/canvas.

24 Guy Melamed, "'Nobody Gets Fired for Buying IBM,'" *Finextra* (blog), May 20, 2024, https://www.finextra.com/blogposting/26205/nobody-gets-fired-for-buying-ibm.

25 Gustavo Razzetti, "The Psychological Safety Bubble: When Too Much Safety Becomes a Hazard," Demystify Culture, July 9, 2023, https://think.fearlessculture.design/p/the-psychological-safety-bubble-when.

26 Ryne Sherman, "Profile," LinkedIn, accessed February 10, 2026, https://www.linkedin.com/in/rynesherman/.

27 Matt Howard and Joshua Cogswell, "The Left Side of Courage: Three Exploratory Studies on the Antecedents of Social Courage," *The Journal of Positive Psychology* 14, no. 3 (January 2018): 1–17. doi:10.1080/17439760.2018.1426780.

28 Jared B. Celniker et al., "Correlates of 'Coddling': Cognitive Distortions Predict Safetyism-Inspired Beliefs, Belief That Words Can Harm, and Trigger Warning Endorsement in College Students," *Personality and Individual Differences*, 185, 0191–8869 (February 2022): https://doi.org/10.1016/j.paid.2021.111243.

29 "CalypsoAI's Insider AI Threat Report: 52% of US Employees Are Willing to Break Policy to Use AI," Calypso AI, August 12, 2025, https://calypsoai.com/news/insider-ai-threat-report/.

30 "Former Best Buy CEO Hubert Joly: Empowering Workers to Create 'Magic,'" *Harvard Business Review*, December 2, 2021, https://hbr.org/2021/12/former-best-buy-ceo-hubert-joly-empowering-workers-tocreate-magic.

Chapter 10: The Collaboration Theater

31 "Pulse Survey: How Collaboration Wins: Leadership, Benefits, and Best Practices," *Harvard Business Review* Analytic Services, 2017, https://hbr.org/resources/pdfs/comm/citrix/HowCollaborationWins.pdf.

32 Brian Mullen, Craig Johnson, and Eduardo Salas, "Productivity Loss in Brainstorming Groups: A Meta-Analytic Integration," *Basic and Applied Social Psychology* 12, no. 1 (1991): 3–23. doi:10.1207/s15324834basp1201_1.

33 Morten Hansen, "When Internal Collaboration Is Bad for Your Company," accessed November 17, 2025, https://www.mortenhansen.com/internal-collaboration-bad-company/.

34 Denver Frederick, "Co-Author of Smarter Collaboration Provides a New Approach for Solving Tough Problems," The Business of Giving, March 29, 2023, https://denver-frederick.com/2023/03/29/co-author-of-smarter-collaboration-provides-a-new-approach-for-solving-tough-problems/.

35 Garrett Cohee and Cora Barnhart, "Often Wrong, Never in Doubt: Mitigating Leadership Overconfidence in Decision-Making," *Organizational Dynamics* 53, no. 3 (2024): 101011. doi.org/10.1016/j.orgdyn.2023.101011.

36 Michelle McQuaid, "Do You Struggle to Ask for Help?" *Psychology Today*, 2016, https://www.psychologytoday.com/us/blog/functioning-flourishing/201607/do-you-struggle-ask-help.

37 Paul J. Zak, "The Neuroscience of Trust," *Harvard Business Review Magazine*, January–February 2017, https://hbr.org/2017/01/the-neuroscience-of-trust.

38 "Decision Making in the Age of Urgency," McKinsey & Company, April 30, 2019, https://www.mckinsey.com/capabilities/people-and-organizational-performance/our-insights/decision-making-in-the-age-of-urgency.

39 "Workslop Is the New Busywork. And It's Costing Millions," BetterUp, accessed November 17, 2025, https://www.betterup.com/workslop.

40 Mark Matousek, "Mary Barra Was Called a 'Lightweight' When She Became CEO of GM—Here's How She Transformed the Company and Silenced Her Doubters," *Business Insider*, January 11, 2018, https://www.businessinsider.com/heres-how-mary-barra-silenced-critics-who-called-her-a-lightweight-2018-1.

Chapter 11: Manage Your Conversational Debt

41 Adam Hayes, "Temporal Discounting: The Psychology Behind Future Reward Depreciation," Investopedia, February 27, 2025, https://www.investopedia.com/temporal-discounting-7972594.

Part III: Reclaim Your Voice
Chapter 13: Regain Conversational Agency

42 "37 Who Saw Murder Didn't Call the Police; Apathy at Stabbing of Queens Woman Shocks Inspector," *New York Times*, March 27, 1964, https://www.nytimes.com/1964/03/27/archives/37-who-saw-murder-didnt-call-the-police-apathy-at-stabbing-of.html.

43 "Bystander Effect," *Psychology Today*, accessed November 12, 2025, https://www.psychologytoday.com/us/basics/bystander-effect.

44 "Ryan versus The White Star Line," BBC News, April 18, 2012, https://www.bbc.com/news/uk-northern-ireland-17612629.

45 Gregory Hall, director, "Secrets of the Dead: Abandoning the Titanic," PBS, November 4, 2020, 55:15, https://www.pbs.org/wnet/secrets/abandoning-titanic-promo/5432/.

46 J. S. Lerner and D. Keltner, "Fear, Anger, and Risk." *Journal of Personality and Social Psychology*, 81, no. 1 (2001): 146–159. https://doi.org/10.1037/0022-3514.81.1.146.

47 Saul McLeod, "Asch Conformity Line Experiment," Simply Psychology, updated May 15, 2025, https://www.simplypsychology.org/asch-conformity.html.

48 Kendra Cherry, "How Groupthink Impacts Our Behavior," Verywell Mind, updated September 23, 2025, https://www.verywellmind.com/what-is-groupthink-2795213.

49 Hannah Rose, "The Abilene Paradox: When Not Rocking the Boat May Sink the Boat," Ness Labs, accessed November 17, 2025, https://nesslabs.com/abilene-paradox.

50 Steven Karpman, "The Karpman Drama Triangle," accessed November 17, 2025, https://karpmandramatriangle.com.

51 Adam Grant, "Instead of Monitoring Employees, Try Motivating Them," *Psychology Today*, September 4, 2013, https://www.psychologytoday.com/us/blog/give-and-take/201309/instead-of-monitoring-employees-try-motivating-them.

Chapter 14: From Surrender to Forward Talk

52 Matt Howard and Joshua Cogswell, "The Left Side of Courage: Three Exploratory Studies on the Antecedents of Social Courage," *The Journal of Positive Psychology* 14, no. 3 (January 2018): 1–17. doi:10.1080/17439760.2018.1426780.

53 Daniel Coyle, "How Showing Vulnerability Helps Build a Stronger Team," Ideas TED, accessed November 17, 2025, https://ideas.ted.com/how-showing-vulnerability-helps-build-astronger-team/.

54 Gustavo Razzetti, "Establish Clear Priorities Using Even Over Statements," Fearless Culture, accessed February 10, 2026, https://www.fearlessculture.design/blog-posts/establish-clear-priorities-using-even-over-statements.

55 Damon Centola, *Change: How to Make Big Things Happen* (Little, Brown Spark, 2021).

56 Laura London, Stephanie Madner, and Dominic Skerritt, "How Many People Are Really Needed in a Transformation?" McKinsey & Company, September 23, 2021, https://www.mckinsey.com/capabilities/transformation/our-insights/how-many-people-are-really-needed-in-a-transformation.

57 "Starting Fires on Purpose—When and How Leaders Need to Break the Rules," First Round, accessed November 17, 2025, https://review.firstround.com/starting-fires-on-purposewhen-and-how-leaders-need-to-break-the-rules/.

Chapter 15: A Forward Talk Culture

58 Gustavo Razzetti, "How to Use Team Rituals to Boost Your Culture," Fearless Culture, accessed November 17, 2025, https://www.fearlessculture.design/blog-posts/how-to-use-team-rituals-to-boost-your-culture.

Part IV: Move Forward
Chapter 18: Forward Talk Practices

59 Gustavo Razzetti, "Uncover the Stinky Fish Canvas," Fearless Culture, accessed November 17, 2025, https://www.fearlessculture.design/blog-posts/uncover-the-stinky-fish-canvas.

60 Bernhard Bockelbrink, James Priest, and Liliana David, "Consent Decision-Making," A Practical Guide to Sociocracy 3.0, updated April 18, 2024, https://patterns.sociocracy30.org/consent-decision-making.html.

Index

D

G

S

About the Author

GUSTAVO RAZZETTI is a culture change instigator, speaker, and CEO of Fearless Culture, a culture design consultancy. He helps leaders build teams that talk about what matters—even when it's uncomfortable.

His real-life insights come from leading more than 1,500 workshops with teams at Mars, Microsoft, Merck, Globant, and the Inter-American Development Bank.

A regular contributor to *Psychology Today*, his work has been featured in *The New York Times*, BBC, and *Forbes*. He is the creator of the Culture Design canvas and author of *Remote, Not Distant* and *Stretch for Change*.

Gustavo helps teams say what everyone's thinking, but no one's saying.

If you want to bring the ideas in this book into your organization, or explore working together, visit gustavorazzetti.com.